THE BUNGALOW BOOK

Floor Plans and Photos of 112 Houses, 1910

HENRY L. WILSON

DOVER PUBLICATIONS, INC.
Mineola, New York

Bibliographical Note

This Dover edition, first published in 2006, is an unabridged republication of
the fifth edition, published by Henry L. Wilson, Chicago, Illinois, 1910.

Library of Congress Cataloging-in-Publication Data

Wilson, Henry L. (Henry Lawrence), b. 1862.
  The bungalow book / Henry L. Wilson.
    p. cm.
  Unabridged republication of the work originally published: 5th ed.
Chicago, Ill. : Henry L. Wilson, 1910.
  ISBN 0-486-45104-6 (pbk.)
    1. Bungalows—United States—Designs and plans. I. Title.

NA7571.W53 2006
728'.3730223—dc22

                         2006046279

Manufactured in the United States of America
Dover Publications, Inc., 31 East 2nd Street, Mineola, N.Y. 11501

THE
BUNGALOW

THE California Bungalow (perhaps so called from its resemblance in its more primitive form to the low-thatched homes of the Bengalese in India) is a direct descendant of the original attempts at architecture in California. It surely can trace its simple artistic lines directly back to the old Missions of the Spanish Padres, and its low overhanging eaves, large porches and general air of hospitality and coziness to the adobe houses of the pioneers. From the "'dobe shacks" of the early settlers to the charming homelike Bungalows of today may seem a long stretch, but it has come along as a steady process of evolution and improvement until today the California Bungalow is known and talked about the world over, and not even the glorious climate and everlasting sunshine call forth from the tourist so many comments of admiration and pleasure as do these cozy homes. California has earthquakes now and then, although happily their severity seems to be moderating as the years roll on, but no doubt the early Spanish Padres had no desire to have tall buildings tumbling on their devoted heads, and for this reason built their houses low and rambling, without, however, sacrificing or abandoning the rather severely plain curves and lines of their old Spanish Mission style. The result was quaint and attractive, and better still, these Mission Bungalows furnished the text which modern architectural skill has amplified and improved, until today we have the perfect Bungalow, a "house beautiful" inside and out, the very embodiment of homelike coziness and convenience, inexpensive, but of refined elegance easily adaptable to almost any location, whether mountain, plain or valley, or on the city's narrow streets, or the broad, shaded village avenues.

In the Bungalow, if properly designed, is combined grace, beauty and comfort at a minimum cost. In its arrangement as set forth in this book, the problem of easy housekeeping and homemaking is reduced almost to an exact science.

California is the home of the modern Bungalow. Its almost constant sunshine makes a house of this fashion a necessity, but there is hardly a town or city in all this broad land where the Bungalow would not prove more attractive than any other style of house. As the "farm house" or the ranch "hacienda," the Bungalow style is ideal.

In the Bungalow is the possibility of combining economy in cost with artistic beauty to an almost unlimited degree. Recognizing this fact long ago, I have for many years directed my best efforts to the perfecting of this style of building, and I take pride in exhibiting the results of my labor and study in the pages of the Bungalow Book, four large editions of which have been completely exhausted in two and a half years.

A notable feature of all my plans is the close symmetrical relation between exteriors and interiors, thus combining graceful outlines with inside convenience and comfort. I find it is a big mistake to adopt a floor plan and then endeavor to fit an exterior to it. Many architects do this, I know, but the result is never satisfactory, and a house so designed is never pleasing to the eye; in fact, it usually attracts attention only by its ugliness. Concessions must be made, and both inside and outside details must be modified to gain that atmosphere of cozy elegance which is so much admired in all of my plans, and I do not feel that my years of study and labor have been all in vain when I receive the expressions of pleasure and commendation from the thousands who have built homes from my designs.

The Bungalow is a radical departure from the older styles of cottage, not only in outward appearance, but in inside arrangement. The straight, cold entrance hall and the stiff, prim, usually darkened parlor have no place in it. Entrance is usually into a large living room—the room where the family gathers, and in which the visitor feels at once the warm, homelike hospitality. Everything in this room should suggest comfort and restfulness. The open fireplace and low, broad mantel, a cozy nook or corner, or a broad window seat, are all means to the desired end. Bookcases or shelves may be fitted into convenient places, and ceiling beams add an air of homely quaintness which never grows tiresome.

Where there is room, I suggest that by all means a den should find a place in your plan. This room need not be large, but its very name is suggestive of luxurious rest amid piles of cushions and surrounded by curios and mementoes which accumulate in every family, each reminiscent of good times gone by. Many one-story Bungalows may have in the attic a den or smoking or billiard room.

The dining room should be large and well lighted, and as it will contain few articles of furniture, it may be finished somewhat elaborately, with paneled wainscoating, plate-rail, etc.

Sleeping rooms should be light and well ventilated, and decorated in rather bright, cheerful tints.

Owing to the comparative smallness of the ordinary bath room, we must strive to arrange the various fixtures in the most economical manner. To dispense with chairs, we might build a seat in some convenient corner. Aside from a medicine cabinet and a linen closet for towels, etc., very little remains to complete this room. For an inexpensive wainscot, hard wall plaster is a suitable alternative for the genuine tile. From the top of the wainscot, which is usually about four feet, a light tint for the walls and ceiling, together with white enameled woodwork, is suggestive of purity and cleanliness, and is very pleasing. Where one can afford decorations, a continuous design of a water scene with lilies and swan thrown in at intervals adds richness to the room.

I am inclined to believe that every housewife who plans a house commences with the kitchen, and I am still more inclined to think she is right. It is a most important room, and should be made as cheerful and convenient as possible. Saving of steps means conservation of energy and health, and consequently promotes the general welfare of the family. Where it is possible, the sink should be in the center of the long drainboard, so that the soiled dishes can be placed at one end and when washed laid on the other. The space underneath the drain-board may be utilized for kitchen utensils. In the modern kitchen much attention is given to the proper distribution of the various cupboards, flour bins, spice receptacles and the many little contrivances which appeal to women. Here, too, the hard wall wainscot, well painted, or, better still, enameled, is valuable from the standpoint of sanitation, as it washes easily and does not absorb dust. White enameled wood work, although more expensive than the natural finish or paint, makes an ideal finish for the kitchen.

PLANS and SPECIFICATIONS

$10.00

Entitles you to a copy of the Wilson Bungalow Book and a complete set of working drawings, details and specifications of any design shown in this book.

WHAT A SET OF PLANS CONSIST OF

A complete set of plans consists of a foundation and cellar plan, floor plans, four elevations and all necessary details; and a complete set of specifications.

The floor plans show the exact size of all rooms, halls, closets, bath rooms, pantries, porches, etc., the location and sizes of all doors and windows; the position of all plumbing fixtures, light fixtures, etc. The details show an elevation and cross section of all exterior and interior trim, such as buffets, mantels, bookcases, seats and medicine cabinets, kitchen and pantry cupboard, flour bins, spice drawers, cooling closets, sinks, draining boards, etc. They also show the construction of beam ceilings, panel wainscoting, as well as sizes and style of all trim, window frames, casement windows, brackets, beams, etc., all figured and drawn to a sufficient scale to enable any carpenter to carry out without the least trouble. The plans are drawn to a quarter of an inch to the foot, and the details are drawn from one-half inch to three inches to the foot, making them sufficiently large to be easily understood.

The specifications are as complete as can be made, great care having been taken to have every item specified, including binding clauses to the contractors, etc.

Duplicate plans and specifications will be furnished for $2.50 per set.

* **Note:** Although complete plans and specifications were offered throughout this book when it was first published in 1910, such plans are no longer available.

No. 137.

Number 137 is one of the most popular designs ever issued from my studio. It has been built many times in Southern California at a cost of about $4,000.00, but it always looks as if it must have cost nearly double that amount. It is a two-story Bungalow of the Swiss Chalet type. It is 36 feet front (not including the porte-cochere) and 40 feet deep, exclusive of the garage at the rear and the tile-floored terrace in front. The Porte-cochere, columns, chimney and exterior walls to belt course is covered with stucco; the walls above belt course are covered with shakes, which are 6 inches wide and 30 inches long, layed 14 inches to the weather. This treatment gives a very artistic effect. If shakes cannot be obtained, shingles may be used instead. Exact dimensions are given on the floor plans, which illustrate many details and should be carefully studied to note the features which have been worked in.

Note also the outline sketch of the interior of living room, with a glimpse of the dining room and stairway platform in the extreme distance. This sketch also gives an idea of the beam-ceiling effect when artistically done. The specifications call for hardwood floors, and beam ceilings in the living room and dining room. Note the very convenient kitchen with separate servants' stairway, the den with gas fireplace and mantel with book shelves on either side, the broad window seat in dining room and buffet in same room, the large open fire-place with seats in living room, etc., etc. See floor plans on next page.

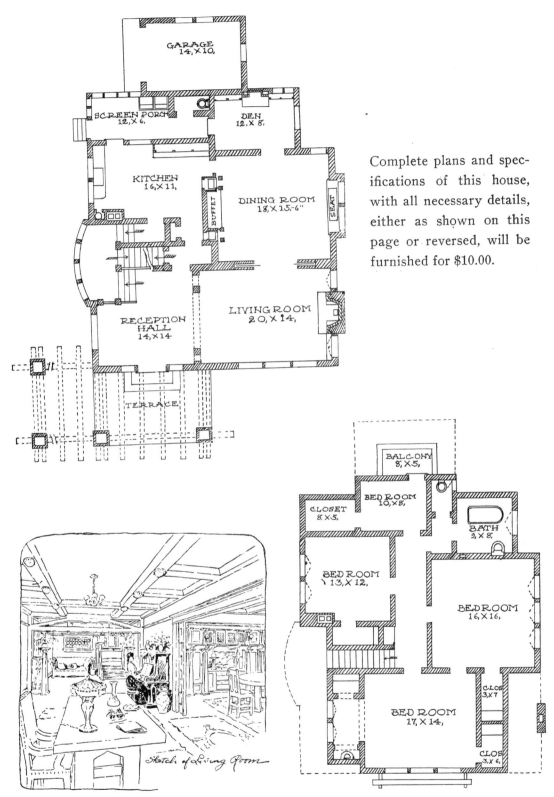

GARAGE
14, X 10,

SCREEN PORCH
12, X 6,

DEN
12, X 8,

KITCHEN
16, X 11,

DINING ROOM
18, X 15,-6"

BUFFET

SEAT

RECEPTION
HALL
14, X 14

LIVING ROOM
20, X 14,

TERRACE

Complete plans and specifications of this house, with all necessary details, either as shown on this page or reversed, will be furnished for $10.00.

Sketch of Living Room

BALCONY
8, X 5,

BED ROOM
10, X 8,

CLOSET
8 X 5,

BATH
9, X 8,

BED ROOM
13, X 12,

BEDROOM
16, X 16,

CLOS
3, X 7

BED ROOM
17, X 14,

CLOS
3, X 6,

Second Floor Plan, No. 137.

7

No. 149.

A very popular design, cozy, homelike and adapted to almost any locality or situation. The rooms are well arranged and the interior is very attractive. This house is 40 feet square over all, and it can be built for about $1,600.

Complete plans and specifications of this house, with all necessary details, either as shown on this page or reversed, will be furnished for $10.00.

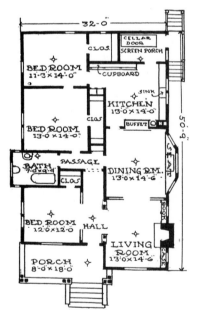

No. 157.

No. 157. To arrange six rooms conveniently seems to be the demand of the general public, and this house is successfully meeting that demand. There is not much waste hall, and yet any room may be entered without interfering with the occupants in the others. For a six-room bungalow this is inexpensive, convenient and attractive. The size is 32 feet by about 51 feet, and its cost is about $1,800.

Complete plans and specifications of this house, with all necessary details, either as shown on this page or reversed, will be furnished for $10.00.

No. 151.

Number 151 has many odd and attractive features. The cobble stone porch with cement steps add to the attractiveness of this Bungalow. The exterior walls are covered with resawed weather - boarding, which may be stained any color to suit owner. The living room and dining rooms have paneled wainscoting, beam ceilings and oak floors, a beautiful buffet in the dining room with leaded glass doors above, a plate mirror over counter shelf and cupboards and drawers below. The buffet kitchen is amply supplied with cupboards, cooling closets, etc. The size of this house is 31x42 feet, not including the porch, and the cost to build is about $1,700.

Complete plans and specifications of this house, with all necessary details, either as shown on this page or reversed, will be furnished for $10.00.

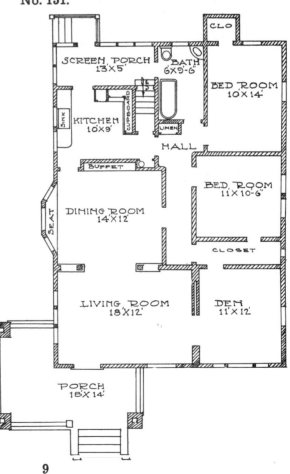

No.158.

Number 158 makes a very desirable seven-room Bungalow. The exterior is very attractive and the interior is so economically arranged as to give much room for comparatively little money. The den, living room and dining rooms have oak floors and panel wainscoting with plate rail at top. The buffet has art glass back, which gives a very good effect. The breakfast room may be used as a sewing room or an extra bed room, as may be desired. The dimensions of this house are 34x46 feet and will cost to build about $1,900.

Complete plans and specifications of this house, with all necessary details, either as shown on this page or reversed, will be furnished for $10.00.

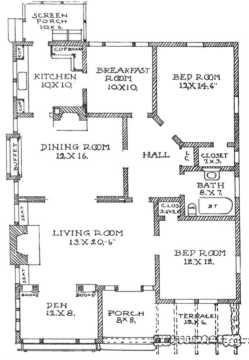

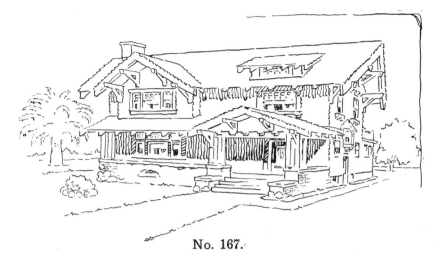

No. 167.

No. 167 is modeled somewhat on the Swiss Chalet style. It is 32 feet front by 45 feet deep, and can be built for about $3,000. Note the buffet kitchen with back stairway, the sun porch opening out of the dining room, the sewing room, the large front piazza, the open brick fireplace in living room with seats on either side, the buffet in dining room, etc. The second floor has four nice chambers and bath room, plenty of closets and a minimum waste of space for hall; in fact, for economical utilizing of space I doubt whether the plan could be surpassed. The exterior of this house is very attractive. The foundation and buttresses of front porch are of clinker brick and cobblestones, and every line and every proportion of the entire structure are exactly right.

Hardwood floors in hall, living and dining rooms. Beam ceiling in hall and living room. Panel wainscoting in living and dining rooms.

Complete plans and specifications of this house, with all necessary details, either as shown on this page or reversed, will be furnished for $10.00.

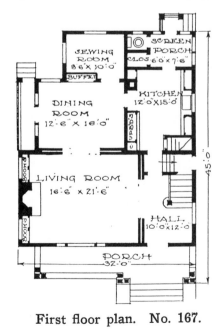

First floor plan. No. 167.

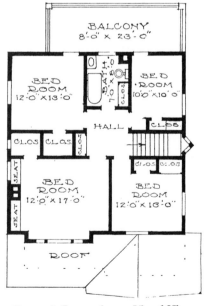

Second floor plan. No. 167.

11

No. 185.

A substantial roomy house, on pure bungalow lines, and not expensive. The rooms are large, light and airy, and it will prove an ideal home for a small family. Size about 40 feet square, and cost about $1,800. The buffet kitchen with sink and cupboards in the bay window is a taking feature.

Complete plans and specifications of this house, with all necessary details, either as shown on this page or reversed, will be furnished for $10.00.

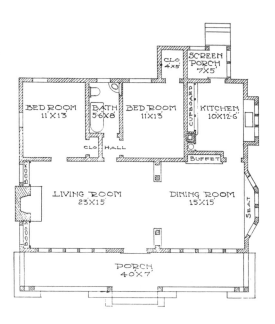

No. 187.

A solid, compact little bungalow, the beauty of which is its almost severely plain lines but well balanced proportions. It looks like a home in every exterior aspect, and the cozy interior strengthens this impression. Size 32 by 46 feet, and will cost about $1,800. The buffet kitchen and pantry are attractive features.

Complete plans and specifications of this house with all necessary details, either as shown on this page or reversed, will be furnished for $10.00.

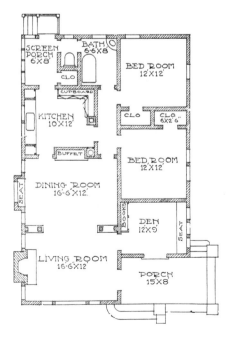

13

No.189.

This cement finished mission Bungalow of seven rooms, exclusive of bath and tower room, is a home that will appeal to many. The rooms are ample in size and admirable in arrangement; especially so for a family entertaining much; the reception hall, the living room and the dining room being arranged en suite, with a floor space of nearly 700 square feet. To this the corner bedroom can be added by throwing open the connecting door. There is a tower room which can be used as an open-air sleeping room, or it can be fitted with windows and used for a bedroom or den. The flat part of the roof can be made into a roof-garden if desired.

The dimensions are 43½ feet front and 44½ feet deep, exclusive of porch and nook, etc., and it should be built for about $3,000, with beamed ceilings in the three principal rooms.

Complete plans and specifications of this house, with all necessary details, either as shown on this page or reversed, will be furnished for $10.00.

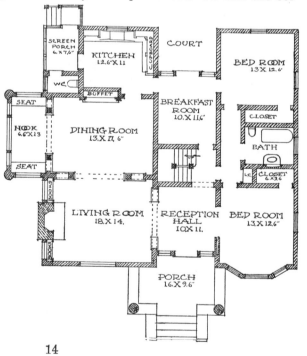

14

No. 190.

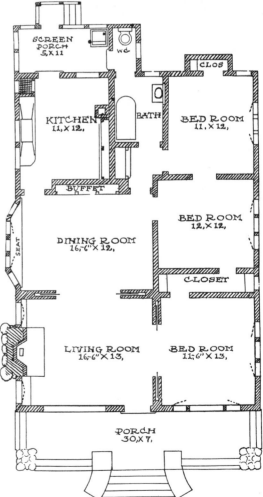

No. 190. For a six-room house, perhaps this is the plan which I most frequently suggest, and never has it failed to bear out my recommendation. Its exterior is massive, solid and artistic. The broad span of the front, the heavy cobblestone pillars, foundation walls and exposed chimney, in connection with the overhanging eaves and shed-roof dormer, all add artistic beauty.

With vines covering the stone work and arches, and shrubbery about the foundations walls, it would be difficult to conceive of a more beautiful home. The interior is quite as attractive, and convenient to the last degree. The living room has broad open fireplace, with cobblestone mantel, beam ceiling, hardwood floor and panel wainscot. Dining room has floors, ceiling, etc., to match living room. Size of house, 30 feet front by 47 feet deep, and can be built for about $2,350.

Complete plans and specifications, $10.00.

15

No. 195.

No. 195. Nothing is more offensive to good taste in architecture than too much "gingerbread" trimming, but the artistic introduction of heavy roof brackets, flower boxes and overhanging shed-roofs greatly enhance the attractiveness of this beautiful and very popular home.

A pleasing effect is produced by the irregular boulders in the exposed brick chimney. Note the convenient, roomy interior, the abundance of closets, the open fireplace, with book shelves on each side, etc. Instead of a conventional buffet, the dining room has a china closet each side of window ledge. This house is 24 feet front by 41 feet deep, and with hardwood floors and beam ceilings in hall, dining and living rooms, has been built for $2,500.00.

Plans and specifications, $10.00.

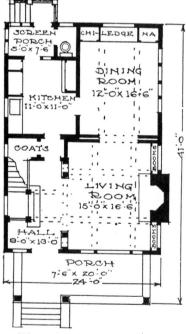

First floor plan. No. 195.

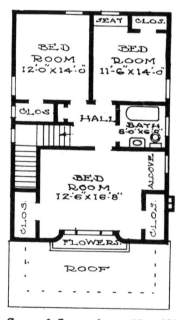

Second floor plan. No. 195.

16

No. 196.

A charming little home for a 50-foot, or wider, lot. The outside construction is rough finish with shakes on the walls. Shingles or weatherboarding can be used if preferred. The piano alcove could be used for a den or office.

This house is 38 feet front, including nook, and about 50 deep, including front porch, and will cost about $1,800.

Complete plans and specifications of this house with all necessary details, either as shown on this page or reversed, will be furnished for $10.00.

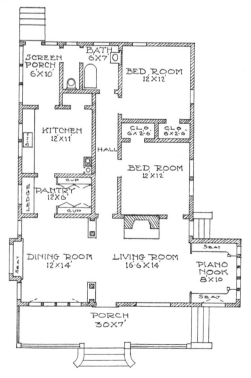

No. 208.

No. 208. Coziness is the keynote to this charming home with many of the advantages of a more stately mansion. Expensive features are supplanted by economical necessities. The arrangement is fine, and in every way conducive to saving of steps. Size 33 feet front by 38 feet deep, and cost about $1,500. The exterior may be either shingles or weatherboarding. The large exposed chimney may be of plain dark burnt brick or clinker brick, with equally good effect.

Complete plans and specifications of this house with all necessary details, either as shown on this page or reversed, will be furnished for $10.00.

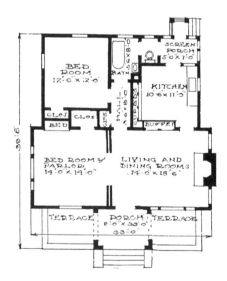

No. 257.

This cozy little Bungalow, containing five rooms, is just the thing for a small family, and can be built for $1,400 or $1,500, depending upon the elaboration of its interior finish. If the principal rooms have oak floors and beamed ceilings, the latter figure will be about right. Interior finish of pine slash-grain for the principal rooms and plain for the others.

Size of Bungalow 36x33 feet over all.

Complete plans and specifications of this house, with all necessary details, either as shown on this page or reversed, will be furnished for $10.00.

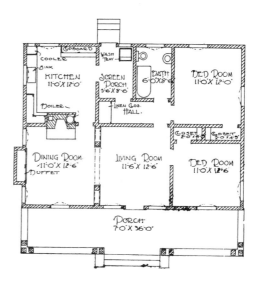

19

No. 310.

Clinker brick, shingled or re-sawed weatherboarding and shingle roof is the construction of this beautiful Bungalow. The kitchen is small but has a fine buffet pantry; size 30 by 51 feet, and will cost about $1,800.

Complete plans and specifications of this house with all necessary details, either as shown on this page or reversed, will be furnished for $10.00.

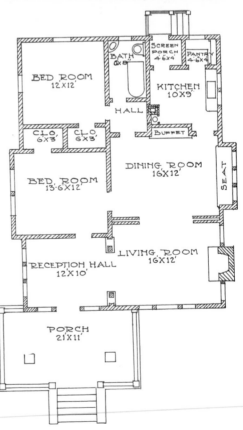

No. 357.

Number 357 has a pleasing exterior and a very attractive interior. It is 32 feet front by 48 feet deep (not including back porch), and can be built for about $2000.00, with hardwood floors and beam ceilings in the living and dining rooms. It has two open fireplaces, buffet kitchen and large screen porch. The connection between kitchen, dining room and hall is very cleverly arranged. The dining room is a beautiful octagonal apartment, and lends itself to tasteful furnishing and decorating. The buffet in the dining room is unusual in design, and has a stained glass window back in dull, well-blended colors, much enhancing the attractiveness of the array of dishes, glass and silverware. In every way I can recommend this house to every lover of a snug, artistic home.

Complete plans and specifications of this house, with all necessary details, either as shown on this page or reversed, will be furnished for $10.00.

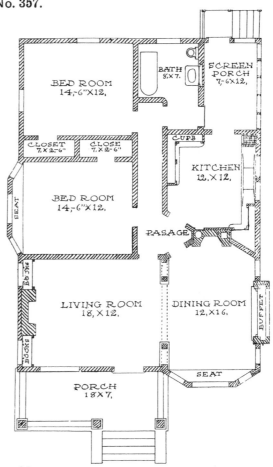

No. 358.

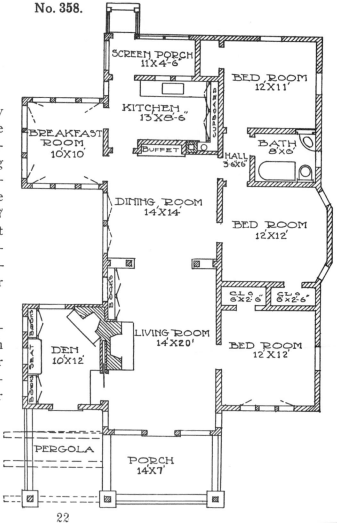

The picture of this classy little Bungalow was made before it was quite completed. It is a charming little nest, and the room arrangement will repay a close inspection. Size 38 by 57 feet, and will cost about $2400.00. This house is particularly adapted to the requirements of a physician or other professional man.

Complete plans and specifications of this house, with all necessary details, either as shown on this page or reversed, will be furnished for $10.00.

SCREEN PORCH
11'X4'-6"

KITCHEN
13'X8'-6"

BED ROOM
12'X11'

BREAKFAST ROOM
10'X10'

BUFFET

BATH
8'X6'

HALL
3'6"X6'

DINING ROOM
14'X14'

BED ROOM
12'X12'

BOOKS

CLO.
6'X2'-6"

CLO.
6'X2'-6"

LIVING ROOM
14'X20'

DEN
10'X12'

BED ROOM
12'X12'

BOOK SEAT

PERGOLA

PORCH
14'X7'

No. 372.

A good substantial home, with every requisite for comfort. This plan is well adapted to the seashore, but quite as suitable for any location. The music room opens out of the living room and has two high windows over the space for piano. Of course, if so desired, this room could be used for a den, or, with slight alteration, as an extra bed room. The features are well shown on the floor plan, and hardwood floors and paneled wainscot are provided for in the music, living and dining rooms.

The house is 28 feet front by 54 feet, and can be built for about $1,800. The picture was made from a newly finished house, and the imagination must supply flowers, trees, shrubbery, vines, etc. In fact, this remark applies to many of the exteriors illustrated in this book.

Complete plans and specifications of this house, with all necessary details, either as shown on this page or reversed, will be furnished for $10.00.

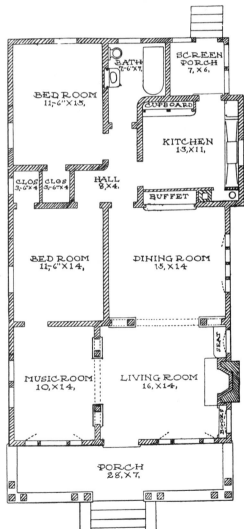

No. 373.

A charming house for any locality, but especially adapted to the hot midday sun of Arizona and adjacent states. If any house can be cool under any conditions, this, with its broad tile roof and hollow tile walls will surely be so. The floor plans are especially good, and I recommend this house in all confidence for any climate.

Size without porch extension, 34 by 40 feet, and can be built for about $4,000. This house can also be built of brick or concrete, but hollow tiles are always dry, cool in summer, warm in winter, and sanitary and healthful at all times.

Complete plans and specifications of this house with all necessary interior details, either as shown on this page or reversed, will be furnished for $10.00.

See floor plans on next page.

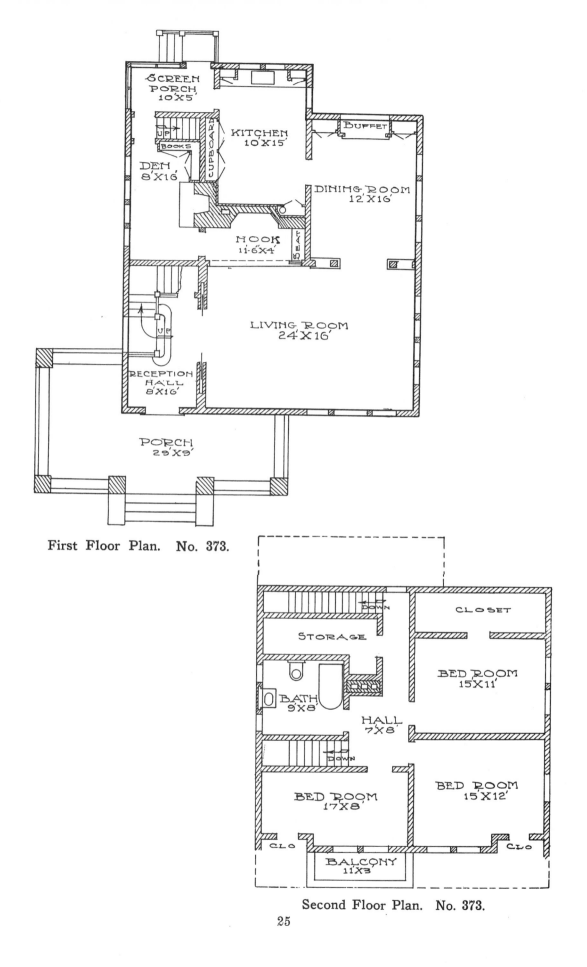

First Floor Plan. No. 373.

Second Floor Plan. No. 373.

25

No. 382.

This is a typical Bungalow, with low roof, broken by long shed dormer, wide overhanging eaves and gables, battered side walls to the belt course, exposed chimney and fine large front porch. It is 30 feet by 52 feet over all, and can be built for about $1,900.00. The interior may well be considered a model plan. Note the fireplace, with seats, and the broad window seat, with book shelves in the living room; wide buffet, bay window and ledge in dining room, convenient arrangement of rear rooms with separate toilet and bath; screen porch with wash trays; large buffet kitchen, etc. Kitchen has a separate chimney, which does not show on floor plan.

Complete plans and specifications of this house, with all necessary details, either as shown on this page, or reversed, will be furnished for $10.00.

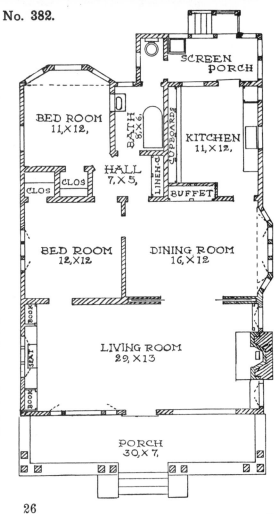

No. 387.

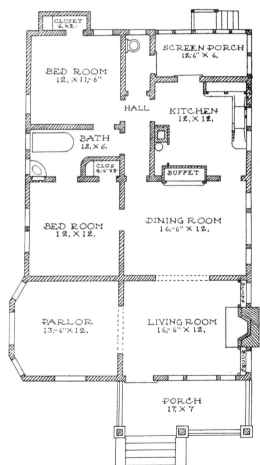

This is an inexpensive house in the best meaning of the term. It has very pretty exterior lines, broken artistically by large brackets, window boxes, etc.; a good roomy porch with brick foundation and pillars. Clinker brick may be used if desired.

The floor plan is self-explanatory. Note the open fireplace with book shelves under the high windows on either side; the large buffet in dining room; the handy kitchen and screen porch; convenient bath room, etc. This plan shows a parlor, but this could readily be arranged for a bed room or den if desired. The house is 30 feet by 44 feet, and can be built for about $1,675.00.

Complete plans and specifications of this house, with all necessary details, either as shown on this page, or reversed, will be furnished for $10.00.

No. 389.

No. 389. A beautiful little Bungalow, which is peculiarly adapted to vines, flowers and shrubbery. Its solid exterior with massive brick chimney, terrace porch and broad bay window opening from living room are very attractive features.

The arrangement of the rooms is excellent. Note the cozy seats in hall and two main rooms, the large buffet in dining room, the very handy buffet kitchen, the position of the bath room between the bed rooms, with separate toilet, etc. This house is 28 feet by 50 feet, and can be built for about $1,600.

Complete plans and specifications of this house with all necessary details, either as shown on this page or reversed, will be furnished for $10.00.

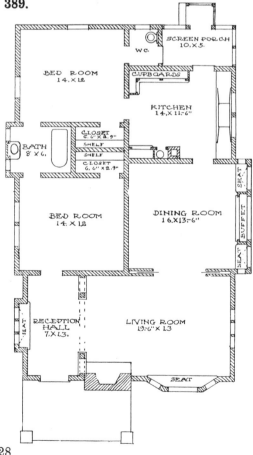

No. 390.

A good substantial home, with every requisite for comfort. This plan is well adapted to the seashore, but quite as suitable for any location. The music room opens out of the living room and has one high window over the space for piano. Of course, if so desired, this room could be used for a den, or, with slight alterations, as an extra bed room. The features are well shown on the floor plan, and hardwood floors and paneled wainscot are provided for in the music, living and dining rooms.

The house is 28 feet front by 44 feet, and it can be built for about $1,600.00.

Complete plans and specifications of this house, with all necessary details, either as shown on this page or reversed, will be furnished for $10.00.

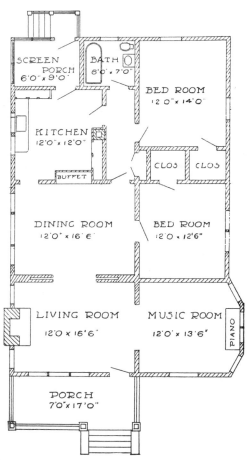

See floor plans on next page.　No. 395.

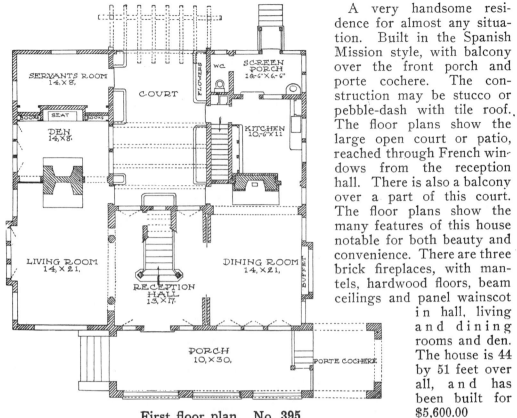

A very handsome residence for almost any situation. Built in the Spanish Mission style, with balcony over the front porch and porte cochere. The construction may be stucco or pebble-dash with tile roof. The floor plans show the large open court or patio, reached through French windows from the reception hall. There is also a balcony over a part of this court. The floor plans show the many features of this house notable for both beauty and convenience. There are three brick fireplaces, with mantels, hardwood floors, beam ceilings and panel wainscot in hall, living and dining rooms and den. The house is 44 by 51 feet over all, and has been built for $5,600.00

First floor plan. No. 395.

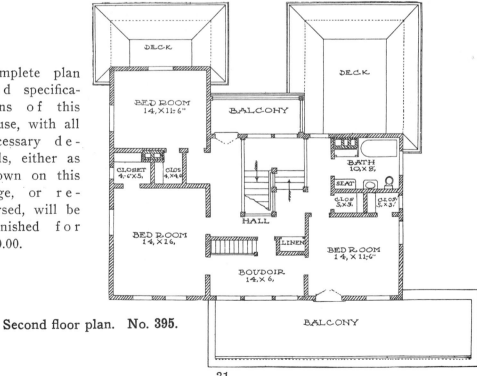

Complete plan and specifications of this house, with all necessary details, either as shown on this page, or reversed, will be furnished for $10.00.

Second floor plan. No. 395.

No. 397.

This two-story Bungalow is admirable in many ways. The cut gives a very good idea of its handsome exterior. The rooms are large and well arranged, and the house has proved a great favorite, having been built many times in Southern California. The floor plans are self-explanatory, and the many attractive features are worthy of careful study. Hardwood floors, beam ceilings and panel wainscoting are provided for in the reception hall, living and dining rooms. The house is 32 feet square, and it can be built for about $3,500.

See floor plans on next page.

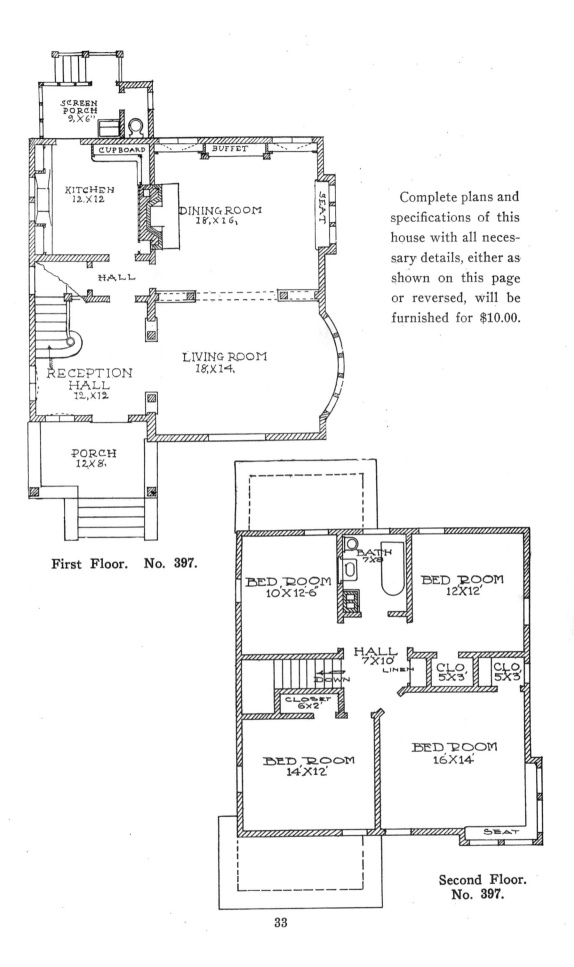

SCREEN PORCH
9,X6"

CUPBOARD

BUFFET

KITCHEN
12.X12

DINING ROOM
18,X16,

SEAT

HALL

LIVING ROOM
18,X14,

RECEPTION HALL
12,X12

PORCH
12,X8,

Complete plans and specifications of this house with all necessary details, either as shown on this page or reversed, will be furnished for $10.00.

First Floor. No. 397.

BED ROOM
10'X12-6"

BATH
7X8

BED ROOM
12X12'

HALL
7X10'

LINEN

CLO.
5X3'

CLO.
5X3'

DOWN

CLOSET
6X2'

BED ROOM
14'X12'

BED ROOM
16'X14'

SEAT

Second Floor. No. 397.

33

No. 406.

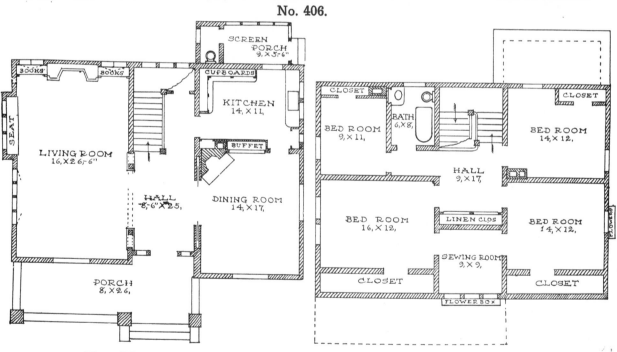

First Floor. No. 406.

Second Floor. No. 406.

The size of this house is 41 feet by 34 feet. Estimated cost is $3,500.

Complete plans and specifications of this house with all necessary details, either as shown on this page or reversed, will be furnished for $10.00.

34

No. 409.

This house, although it can be built at very small cost, is attractive as to exterior with fair sized rooms and as many conveniences as could reasonably be expected at the figure. There is no bath-room. There is only one bed-room, but a wall bed can be built in the living-room if desired, giving additional sleeping facilities. The porch is nice and wide.

The bungalow can be built for $800.

Complete plans and specifications of this house, with all necessary details, either as shown on this page or reversed, will be furnished for $10.00.

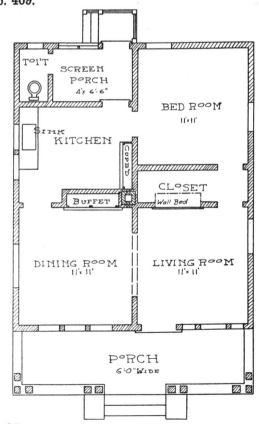

35

No. 414.

This is a Colonial cottage without the exterior Bungalow features. It has proved most satisfactory every time it has been built, and for a large, convenient, handsome home, I recommend it strongly. It is 34 feet front by 54 feet deep, and has been built for $3,500. It has hardwood floors in living room and dining room, with paneled wainscoting. The living room has beam ceiling, pressed brick mantel and fireplace, with book shelves, etc. The balcony in front of second story is large enough for sleeping, and is a well liked feature, as is also the maid's room directly over the kitchen, with back stairs, which also communicate with the main second-story hall. Closets, pantries, buffet and cupboard are all shown on the plan, which should be studied closely. The large front porch is ample for a camping ground for all the family and half the neighbors. See floor plans on next page.

See floor plans on next page.

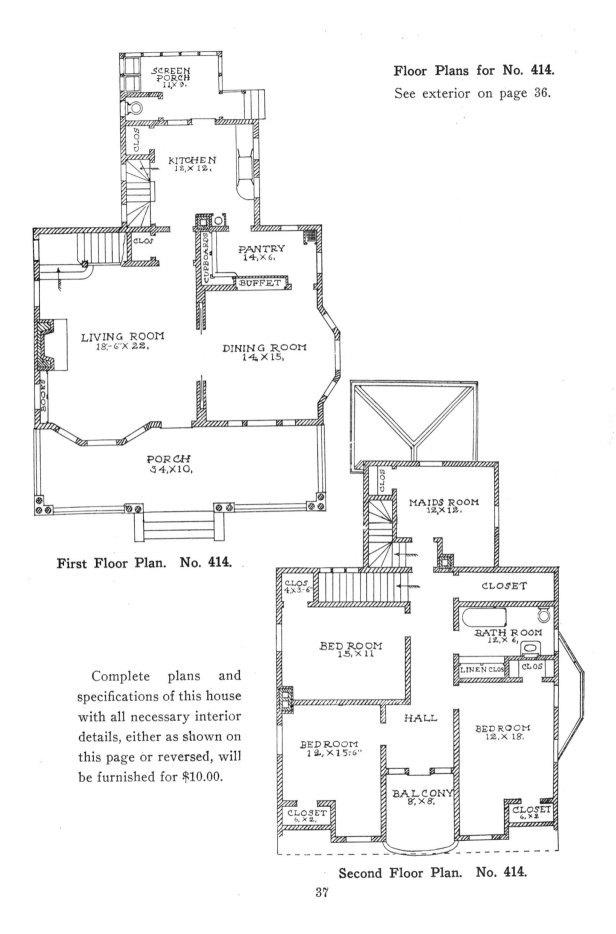

SCREEN PORCH
11×9.

CLOS

KITCHEN
12,×12,

CLOS

PANTRY
14,×6,

CUPBOARDS

BUFFET

LIVING ROOM
18,-6"×22,

DINING ROOM
14,×15,

BOOKS

PORCH
34,×10,

First Floor Plan. No. 414.

CLOS

MAIDS ROOM
12,×12,

CLOS
4×3-6"

CLOSET

BED ROOM
15,×11

BATH ROOM
12,×6,

LINEN CLOS   CLOS

HALL

BED ROOM
12,×18.

BED ROOM
12,×15-6"

BALCONY
8,×8,

CLOSET
6,×2,

CLOSET
6,×2,

Complete plans and specifications of this house with all necessary interior details, either as shown on this page or reversed, will be furnished for $10.00.

Second Floor Plan. No. 414.

37

No. 419.

This house is 30 feet 10 inches in front and 27 feet 10 inches in the rear, and 50 feet 6 inches in length, including porches. There are four large rooms upon the first floor, and three in the half-story above, in addition to staircase halls, screen porch and bath room.

The living room has a handsome pressed brick mantel and book cases with leaded glass doors, and the dining room a recessed buffet with slide opening to kitchen, and a long window seat under the triple side windows. Both living room and dining room have beamed ceilings (if desired) and are separated by broad sliding doors.

The staircase hall communicates with the living room, the bedroom and the kitchen, and is well lighted by a window upon the half-landing.

The bedroom upon the first floor may be used as a sewing room, if provided with gas fuel, or other means of heating. It has a closet under the stairs, and communicates with the screen porch through a toilet.

The kitchen is large and fitted up with a sink, a cooler, two flour bins, four dwarf closets, ample cupboards with doors, and nearly twenty lineal feet of counter top cases and drip-boards.

The half-story above contains three large bed rooms; those in front lighted from two sides, and open out upon a balcony through glass doors. They also have window seats with hinged tops. All have closets of good

38

size fitted with shelves and hooks. There is also a linen closet in the hall with drawers beneath.

The bath room is of very large size and in addition to the lavatory, tub and toilet has a medicine cabinet and a good closet.

There is an unfinished store room opening out of the rear bed room, suitable for the storage of empty trunks, etc., and there is ample space for an attic of over 650 square feet of floor area, if a floor is laid and means of access provided. This can be done by means of a scuttle in the hall ceiling near the linen closet—that part of the ceiling being dropped to a height of 7 feet 2 inches for convenience in using a step-ladder. The balance of the ceilings are 8 feet 6 inches in the chamber story and 9 feet below.

Built upon brick foundations, re-sawed siding walls and stained shingle roof; oak floors and beamed ceilings for principal rooms, etc., the cost is about $3,000. Cellar stairs may go down under main stairs from hall.

Complete plans and specifications of this house, with all necessary details, either as shown on this page or reversed, will be furnished for $10.00.

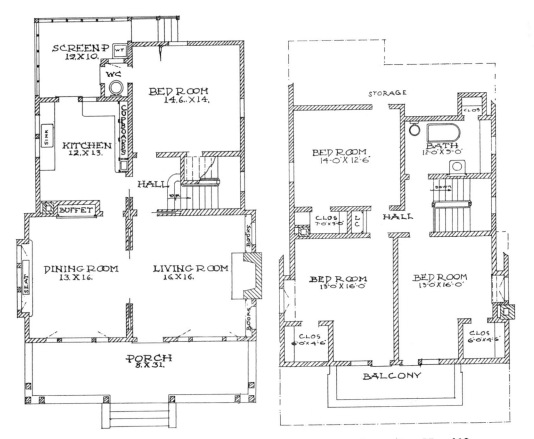

First floor plan No. 419.   Second floor plan No. 419.

39

No. 420.

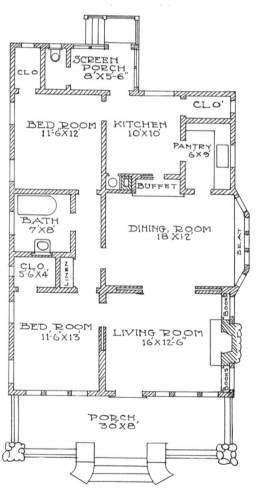

This handsome Bungalow has many commendable features and has been built a dozen times or more, always giving complete satisfaction. The broad span of the front porch affords an unobstructed view from the large living room. The construction is resawed weatherboarding, shingle roof, cobble chimney and porch columns, etc. Clinker brick or hard dark red brick can be used instead of cobbles with good effect. There is a fine buffet kitchen, and the bath room arrangement is excellent.

The size is 30 feet by 47 feet and with hardwood floors, beam ceilings and panel wainscot in living and dining rooms, the cost will be about $2,400.

Complete plans and specifications of this house with all necessary interior details, either as shown on this page or reversed, will be furnished for $10.00.

No. 429.

The rustic nature of clinker brick makes it a splendid surface over which to train vines.

In No. 429 clinker brick has been used for the foundation of the porch and the chimney. This illustration is a convincing argument that the California bungalow is well adapted to use as a country home, in eastern surroundings.

The entrance is by way of a small reception hall; a den with book-cases is to the left; to the right is the living room which has a battan wainscot around the room, at the height of the column buttress, and the mantel shelf, which is of heavy proportions, over wood brackets, upon a facing of pressed brick. The crown mould of the head casings of the doors and windows continues around the room, as a picture mould.

A seat is built in the dining room bay window. The buffet is broad, extending to the cross beams of the ceiling.

A pass pantry, that could be omitted, is located in the corner of the kitchen. Bins opening into the kitchen are built in the pantry cupboard.

This bungalow is 30 by 65 feet over all, and would cost approximately $2,500.

Complete plans and specifications of this house, with all necessary details, either as shown on this page, or reversed, will be furnished for $10.00.

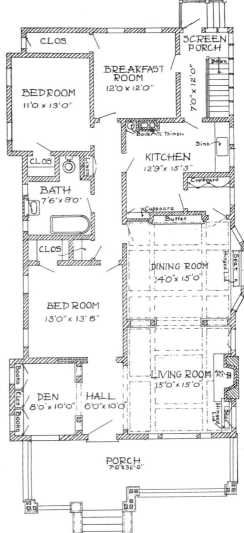

No. 437.

Cobblestones used for the porch and chimneys form the principal color note in the exterior of No. 437. The triple windows of the den, supplied with a flower box, add charm to the front elevation. Sliding doors separate the living room from the den and dining room. Clinker brick and cobblestones are used with very successful result in building the fireplace, which has book-cases on each side.

Large closets and bedrooms are excellent qualities, included in this plan. The rear hall has a closet for linen.

Cupboards and broom closet are built in the kitchen. A hinged bin is provided for the space under the sink drain-board. $2,400 would build No. 437, which is 32 by 55 total dimensions.

Complete plans and specifications of this house, with all necessary details, either as shown on this page or reversed, will be furnished for $10.00.

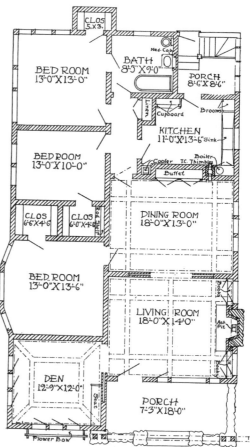

No. 438.

No. 438 is a good example of a large, roomy house at moderate cost. Every room is large, light and airy, and there is not an inch of waste space. The house is 30 feet front by 52 feet deep, and with beam ceilings and hardwood floors in living and dining rooms can be built for about $1,950.00. The exterior, with its well proportioned lines, is very attractive, and the floor plans will repay careful examinations. Note the broad brick fireplace and mantel with book shelves on either side; the window seat in the dining room, the butler's pantry between dining room and kitchen, and the small dressing room opening from the rear bed room. A most satisfactory house in every respect.

Complete plans and specifications of this house, with all necessary details, either as shown on this page or reversed, will be furnished for $10.00.

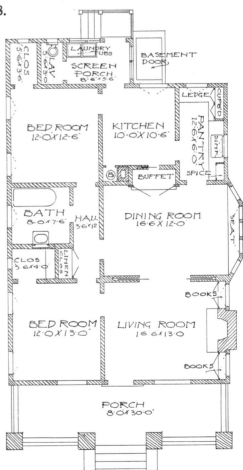

43

No. 443.

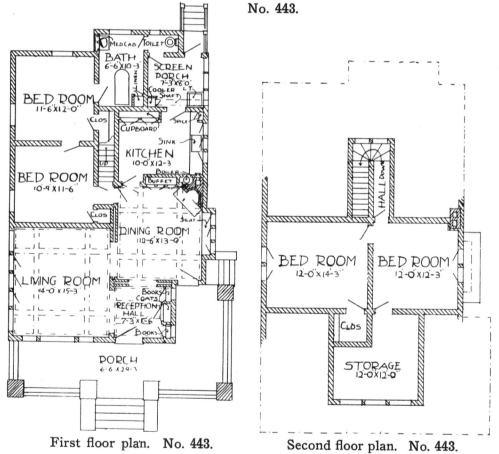

First floor plan. No. 443.　　　Second floor plan. No. 443.

This artistic bungalow has oak floors, panel wainscoting and beam ceilings in reception hall, living room and dining room. Size over all is 28 by 45 and will cost about $2,000.

Complete plans and specifications, $10.00.

No. 445.

This is an inexpensive and attractive little home. Resawed rustic siding for the exterior walls and brick for the porch and chimneys give it durability and charm.

Wood battens are used to divide the walls of the living room and dining room into panels of plaster. Chamfered columns, placed in the arch, extend up five feet high to the height of the wainscot cap. Lights or jardinieres, etc., may be used as a decoration, supported by the columns.

The head casing of the openings continue around the room with shelf and brackets uniting the dining room buffet and mantel. This house is 32 by 43 feet. $1,700 would build it as described.

Complete plans and specifications of this house, with all necessary details, either as shown on this page or reversed, will be furnished for $10.00.

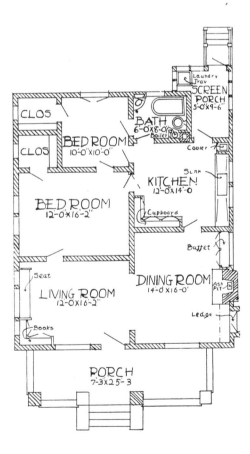

No. 446.

This pleasing but unpretentious little bungalow was built from our plan No. 446. Persons who prefer a conservative design would admire this plan because it partakes more of the conventionality of the Colonial style; particularly noticeable is this in the form of the porch balustrade, which although not truly conforming to any Colonial example, yet has the same basic principle of symmetry of design.

Shingles form the wall of the gable, which is supported by brackets under the projection.

Resawed rustic siding is used on the walls.

This floor plan will meet the favor of those who do not wish to have a direct entrance into the living room; a small entrance hall is partly screened from the living room by columns and buttresses, which may be omitted by any builder if it is desired to throw the entrance hall and living room into one room. The dimensions of this house are 34 by 49 feet, not including rear porch, and can be built for about $1,900.

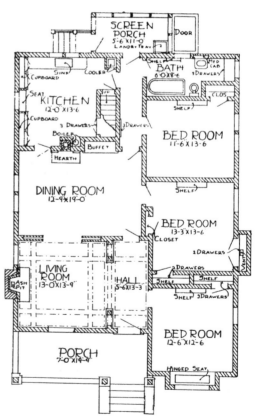

Complete plans and specifications of this house with all necessary details, either as shown on this page or reversed, will be furnished for $10.00.

No. 448.

A simple, dignified home that would disappoint minds seeking something startling and unusual in design.

A roomy porch is crossed to enter the reception hall, which the owner desired to be provided with sliding doors. A broad expanse of fireplace is executed upon the same generous lines of the dining room buffet. The chambers are roomy and have adequate closet space; 44 by 60 is the area of this plan.

Resawed siding is used on the exterior walls, oak floors are specified in the rooms with beamed ceilings.

The cost of this home would approximate $2,600.

Complete plans and specifications of this house, with all necessary details, either as shown on this page or reversed, will be furnished for $10.00.

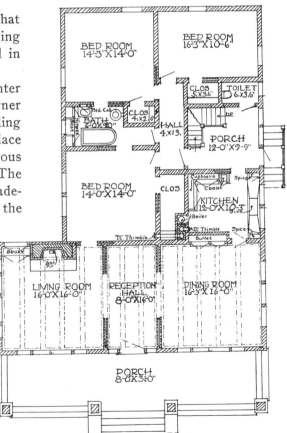

No. 451.

A modest six-room bungalow with requisite accommodations for a family of four or more persons. The front hall serves as a vestibule for the three front rooms—a feature that many will appreciate. This makes the first and second rooms upon the right hand side available as sitting room and bed room to be rented to some acceptable person or party, in case one bed room will suffice for the owner. A closet may be provided for the first room if considered as more valuable than the separate dining room entrance from the hall, and the toilet can be put in the bath room if preferred to the present arrangement or in addition thereto, at a small additional expense. This bungalow is 28 by 42 and can be built for about $1,400 to $1,600, according to the interior finish.

Complete plans and specifications of this house, with all necessary details, either as shown on this page or reversed, will be furnished for $10.00.

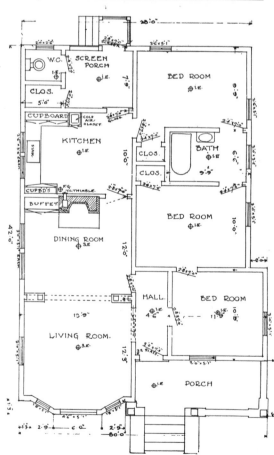

No. 461.

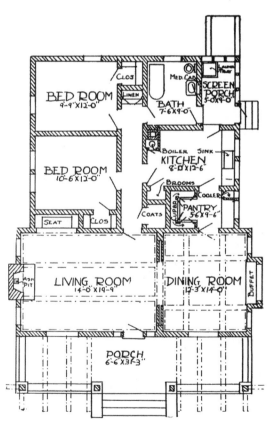

The light and airy effect of the exterior, due to the pergola terraces at either side of the entrance, is as beneficial to the living room as to the front view. We think the value of a front porch, entirely roofed, may be overestimated.

In this instance, the overhanging gable over the entrance, very pleasing of itself, also gives the required covered entrance-way in stormy weather. This, in connection with vines on the beams and awnings, if desired, gives all the needed protection from sun or wind that would be required during the weather conditions when a living porch would be used in any climate.

This house is 32 by 42, and will cost $1,700.

Complete plans and specifications of this house, with all necessary details, either as shown on this page or reversed, will be furnished for $10.00.

No. 463.

No. 463 is an exceptionally pretty design and lends itself peculiarly well to vines and flowers. The square part of front porch has been used as a lovely outdoor sitting room in each instance when the house was built. The features are many; the reception hall with seat, the three open fireplaces, the cozy den, with book shelves, the large living room with corner seats, etc. Back stairs go up from the screen porch to the large storage room. Hardwood floors, beam ceilings and panel wainscot are planned for the living and dining rooms and reception hall; and the house, which is 38 by 48 feet, can be built for about $2,250.

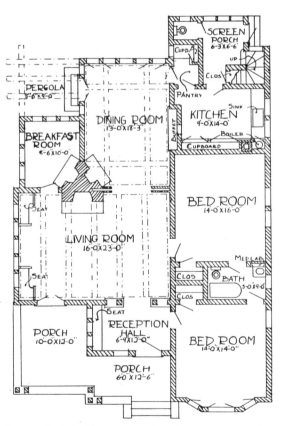

Complete plans and specifications of this house, with all necessary details, either as shown on this page or reversed, will be furnished for $10.00.

No. 465.

This is one of the most pleasing bungalows presented in this number. Its lines are embodiments of cosiness, hospitality and all that one could wish in a diminutive home. The pergola beams, supported on plastered columns, make a splendid place over which vines may grow and add to the charm.

The porch floor is wood, but the front step is brick, as may be seen in this view. A welcome variation from the customary balusters is shown in the vertical jointed and pierced boards of the porch. Resawed siding is used for the outside walls and gables.

The small glass in the front door is plate. Asbestos roofing has been used very appropriately.

The interior also shows the result of striving for economy and convenience. On page 142 may be found a drawing of the buffet of this pleasing little bungalow. Note the economy attained by combining dining-room and kitchen flues in one chimney, also the sanitary wall bed in the dining-room, which gives the bed-room capacity of a five or six-room bungalow.

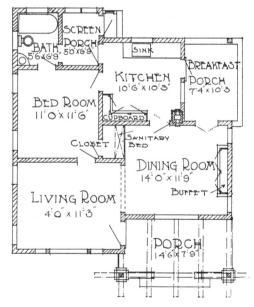

The breakfast porch is ideally located for its purpose; it may be screened to give more privacy or to exclude uninvited, winged guests.

The bath is by no means lacking in ventilation by reason of its corner location.

The width of this plan is 29½ feet; the pergola beams project 3 feet beyond this dimension. The length is 31½ feet, beyond which the pergola beams project 6 feet.

It could be built for $1250.

Complete plans and specifications of this house, with all necessary details, either as shown on this page or reversed, will be furnished for $10.00.

No. 466.

The fact that the entrance porch is comparatively small for a house of this size is compensated by the additional light secured for the den and living room.

Brick masonry for the foundation, porch piers, buttresses and chimneys with cement steps and floor give permanency to the exterior. Resawed rustic siding is used for the weather boarding between the foundation and up to the tops of the windows above which shingles form the covering for the walls and gables.

The cost of this house might be materially reduced by diminishing the height above the grade, which is four feet and two inches.

The front door opens into a reception hall, which gives entry to the den, living room and rear hall, and is equipped with a convenience in the form of a coat closet.

Wood cornices are included in the den, reception hall and living room. This method of treating the ceiling is much cheaper and equally as effective as the built-up beams and are embodied in our latest plans with more pleasure by our draftsmen who are striving for honesty of design.

Considerable originality is displayed in the handling of the pressed brick mantel in the living room and the dining room buffet.

The basement stairway descends under the stairway to the second floor, which contains two large bed rooms with large closet space. No. 466 is 36 by 50 feet and would cost $3,000.

Complete plans and specifications of this house, with all necessary details, either as shown on this page or reversed, will be furnished for $10.00.

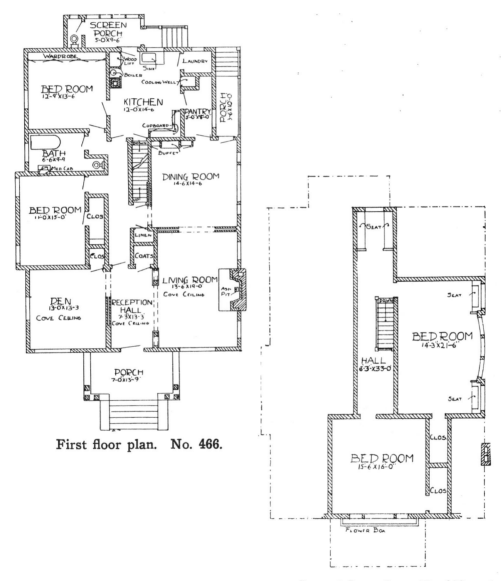

First floor plan. No. 466.

Second floor plan. No. 466.

No. 471.

Clinker bricks form the front porch piers and walls, and are also employed in building the chimneys.

Chains take the place of the usual wood balustrade on the front porch. The front steps are cement, as is the porch floor.

The slight upward trend of the terminations of the ridges forms a peculiar line that is becoming popular with many local builders.

The living room mantel is built with pressed brick, a wide semi-circular arch springing from the "hobs" of the fireplace.

Leaded glass doors are included in the book-cases, on either side of the mantel. Both the living room and the dining room have beam ceilings. Columned buttresses, at the height of the wainscot, divide the front room into a living room and dining room. The three bed rooms and bath room are sufficient to meet the needs of a moderate sized family. The main dimensions of this plan are 30 by 61 feet.

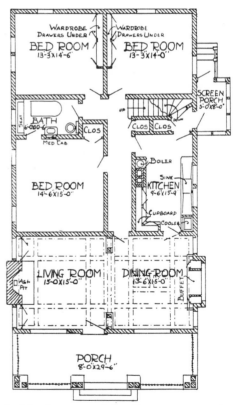

Complete plans and specifications of this house, with all necessary details, either as shown on this page or reversed, will be furnished for $10.00.

No. 476.

Cobblestones form an artistic type of masonry for the porch and foundation. A cobblestone mantel with seats on either side give a good first impression upon entering the living-room, which, like the dining-room, has a beam ceiling.

The dining-room is fitted with a bay window buffet.

The most enthusiastic fresh-air crank would be delighted by the result of this court plan, giving windows on three sides of the kitchen and screen sleeping-room; the hall is benefited by the window inserted upon the court. Over all this house is 39x44 feet and could be built for $2,200.

Complete plans and specifications of this house with all necessary details, either as shown on this page or reversed, will be furnished for $10.00.

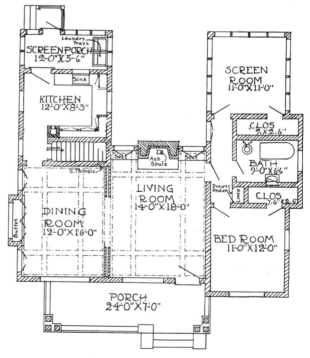

No. 483.

This bungalow has a greater capacity than would be supposed from a view of the exterior. The irregular shape of the porch gives a small space that may be used for a living porch, as it would not be necessary to cross that portion in entering the house.

The bay window in front is covered by the overhanging wall of the gable which is supported on brackets similar to those of the roof. This makes a very effective front elevation. The side gable is given interest by the corbeling, outside chimney, making this side suitable for a corner lot, as the head casing is a continuation of the main beam of the pergola, which makes also a pleasing screen for the windows of the den and dining-room entrance.

A small reception hall is desired by some persons in, preference to a direct entrance into the living-room. This has been provided in this plan, which would also make it possible to use the front bed room as an office or studio, if preferred. Upon entering, an attractive view is obtained from the front of the living-room to the group of windows in the rear of the dining-room. The treatment of the wainscot in this bungalow is unusually good.

The mantel in the living-room is a massive, imposing creation, nearly eight feet wide; a heavy wood shelf, on proportionately large brackets, marks the point at which the projection of the brick mantel is corbeled or stepped, back to the line of the wall above, giving a pyramidal appearance to this portion of the mantel.

The den could be used as a breakfast room, being located alongside of, and in connection with, the dining-room. Many persons will appreciate the manner in which the kitchen is isolated from the remainder of the house. A stairway at this point leads to the basement under the stairway to the second floor. The second floor has a good sized screened sleeping room and a large storage-room, which could be made into a bed room with a very small outlay. The total length from front bed room to rear screen porch is 56 feet. The main width is 40 feet.

The estimated cost of No. 483 is $2,850.

Complete plans and specifications of this house with all necessary details, either as shown on this page or reversed, will be furnished for $10.00.

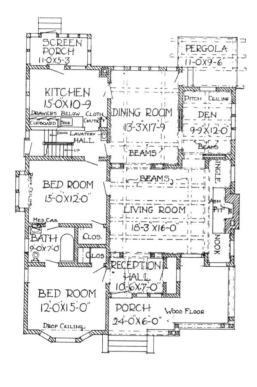

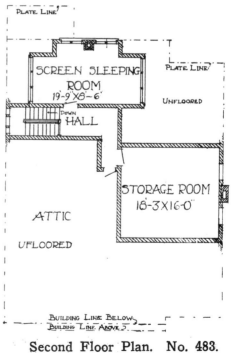

Second Floor Plan. No. 483.

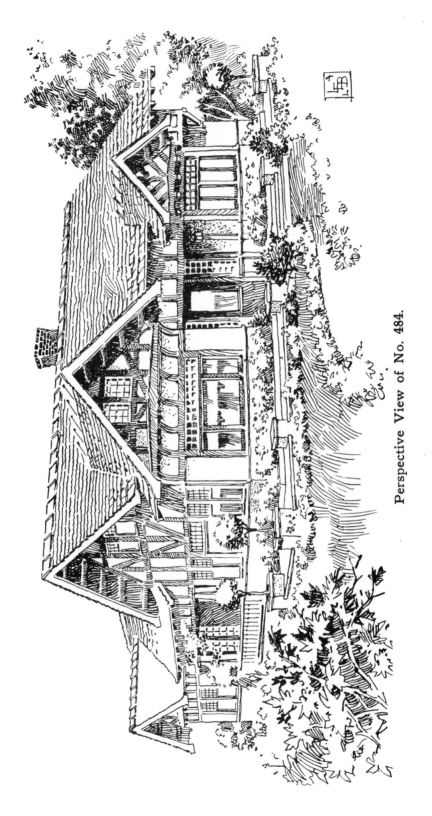

Perspective View of No. 484.

The illustration opposite gives a good idea of the appearance of this half timber and stucco house, which has many characteristics of the English style of domestic architecture.

The main windows are of plate glass. Upon entering, the first point of interest is the ingle-nook; its stone mantel and seats are very carefully executed.

An auxiliary flight of stairs leading from the rear hall gives the advantage of a separate stairway in connection with the main stairway.

The corridor leading from living-room to dining-room is well lighted by the French doors opening upon the recessed side porch.

The dining-room located on the rear is a nearer approach to the European arrangement.

Two bed-rooms and a toilet-room are built upon the second floor. These could be utilized by the members of the family even though a servant be employed, as a maid's room is located on the rear screen porch.

The main body of this house is 36 feet in width; add 4 feet for the rear toilet-room. The length is 56½ feet, to which is added 8½ feet by the maid's room, and 7 feet by the additional projection of the front porch. It could be built for $3,300.

Complete plans and specifications of this house with all necessary details, either as shown on this page or reversed, will be furnished for $10.00.

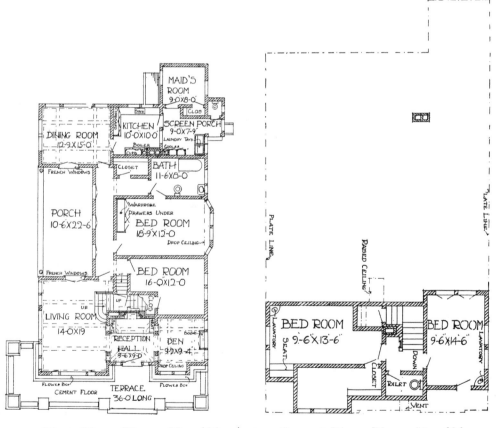

First Floor Plan. No. 484.   Second Floor Plan. No. 484.

No. 486.

This is similar in appearance and plan to designs we have previously published, but offers some variations in external details. The upward sweep of the terminations of the ridge boards, suggestive of the Orient, is admired by many.

Shingles form an appropriate covering for the exterior in this instance. Peculiarly adapted to the irregular bungalow, is the type of masonry here used.

A cosy nook is built in the living-room. Beam ceilings, of simple lines, add to the home-like dining-room and living-room.

A pleasing composition of vertical, plate-glass panels is included in the buffet. Glass doors divided by wood bars, above, and a large beveled plateglass mirror on the counter shelf, contribute to its satisfactory effect.

The front bed-room, with a large bay window and the rear bed-room on the corner, are desirable arrangements.

Thirty-four feet by 60 feet is the total area required by this plan. The cost of building No. 486 would be about $1,900.

Plans and specifications, $10.00.

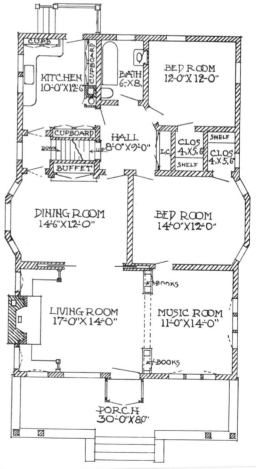

No. 488.

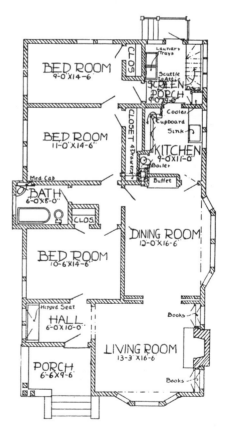

This bungalow was built from our plan No. 488. It was slightly modified in execution, the roof as shown here being slightly lower in pitch than as indicated on the working drawings. The gables are shingled, rustic resawed siding being specified on the walls.

The shelf bay window adds charm to both the exterior and the living-room, which also contains an artistic combination of book-cases and pressed brick mantel.

The dining-room is enlarged by the bay window and fitted with an attractive buffet with the stiles of the panels beveled, in the doors below the counter shelf.

A stairway located on the screen porch, leads to the basement.

No. 488 is 28x53 feet and would cost $1,850.

This plan can also be furnished in stucco as shown here.

Complete plans and specifications of this house with all necessary details, either as shown on this page or reversed, will be furnished for $10.00.

61

No. 492.

A careful inspection of these plans will show many desirable and unusual features. Entering the reception hall from the cement-floored porch, through a handsome four-foot oak door, you are impressed at once with the pleasing and somewhat spacious ensemble that meets your eyes. The stairs lead to a quarter-landing about four feet above the floor, with a slightly projecting bay window and window-seat upon the right hand side, and a low chest-seat upon the left of the short run. Turning your eyes towards the living-room, with its gas fireplace and cozy-corner seat, its plaster-paneled dado and beamed ceiling is before you, seen through the buttressed and square pillared opening separating it from the room you are in;—the two rooms extending entirely across the front of the house, with a fire-place at one end and a bay window at the other. The sliding doors of the dining-room are run back into their pockets, and through the broad opening,—eight feet in width,—you get a fine view of end of the dining-room, entirely open to the light through five windows arranged in a pleasing curve; and through a four-foot sliding doorway at the end of the handsome buffet, you look into the den, and see two built-in bookcases with leaded glass doors, flanking a writing desk; and three small casement windows above them.

You are struck at once with the thought—"What a beautiful arrangement of rooms;—especially for the entertainment of a large company!"

The kitchen is amply provided with cupboards, and a cooling closet. The back-stairs lead up from the kitchen to the landing, leaving a passage to the upstairs or front hall; the cellar stairs also lead from the kitchen to the cellar, the outside cellar door opens off the landing on the side of the house. This house is 28x48, and will cost about $3,500.

See floor plan on next page.

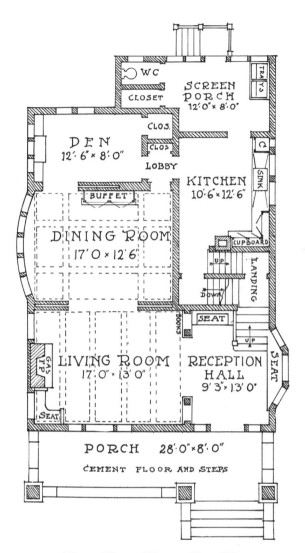

Complete plans and specifications of this house with all necessary details, either as shown on this page or reversed, will be furnished for $10.00.

First Floor Plan. No. 492.

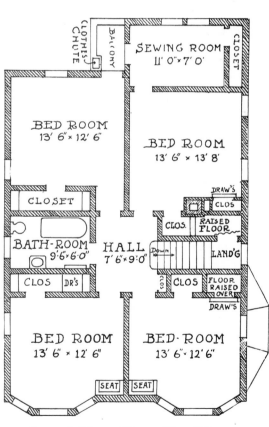

Second Floor Plan. No. 492.

No. 496.

Here is a ten-room two-story house built upon bungalow lines that is at once novel, striking and attractive in exterior design, and of excellent arrangements of room as to plan. The exterior is covered with shakes to second-story windows, and shingles from there up.

The foundation and porch buttresses are built of split stone, which could be clinker brick or boulders if preferred; the porch floor is cement. The floor plan has many admirable features. The plan shows panel wainscoting and beam ceilings in reception hall, living room and dining-room; these features may be omitted if desired. The kitchen is very conveniently arranged with cabinets and dumb waiter from basement; there is also a clothes chute leading from second floor to laundry room in basement. The basement is laid out with a coal room, heating plant room, laundry and vegetable room; the cellar stairs lead down from the passage off from the kitchen. This house is 45 feet 6 inches wide and 26 feet deep, not including front and back porch, and will cost about $3,500.

See floor plan on next page.

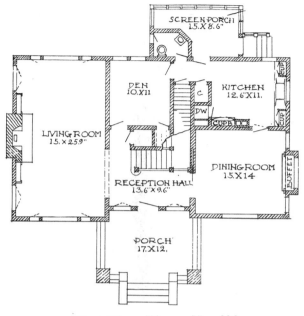

First Floor Plan.   No. 496.

Complete plans and specifications of this house, with all necessary details, either as shown on this page or reversed, will be furnished for $10.00.

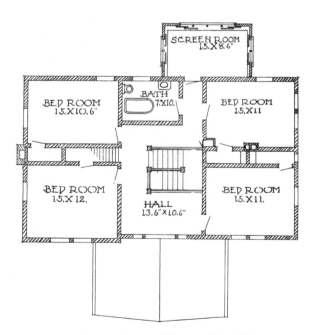

Second Floor Plan.   No. 496.

No. 530.

Construction—Glazed machine-made terra cotta blocks, a new and admirable mode of building, which I commend strongly. (See floor plan on next page.)

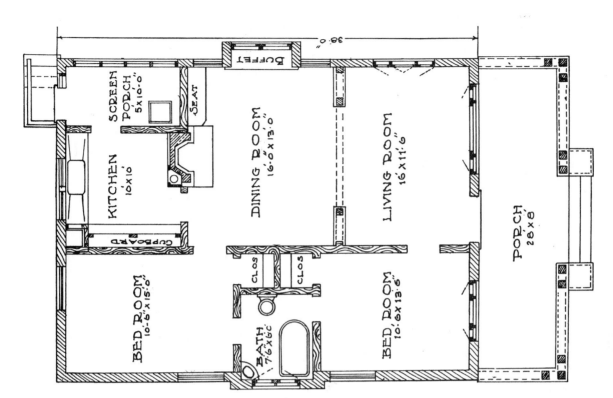

This house is built of glazed machine-made terra cotta blocks, a new method of construction which is in every way commendable and which is becoming very popular. The blocks are made in various shapes and sizes to conform to any demands of architecture. They are hollow, thus insuring warmth in winter and coolness in the heated term, and a dry, healthy home always. The outer surface is a very hard, dull glaze, impervious to rain, requiring no paint, and practically everlasting, while the inside has a rough surface so that no lath is needed and only about one-half the usual amount of plaster. The blocks are made in many colors so that most pleasing effects can be produced. This method of building is cheaper than brick, and in fact, considering the saving of paint, lath, plaster and labor, it will cost but little more than frame and be infinitely better in many ways. I have plans and specifications now ready for this house as shown, and am prepared to execute other designs promptly. This floor plan is simple, but very convenient and roomy, and the house can be built for about $1,800. Size 28 feet by 46 feet.

Complete plans and specifications of this house with all necessary interior details, either as shown on this page or reversed, will be furnished for $10.00.

67

No. 533.

This Mission design makes a very attractive home; the exterior walls are of cement stucco, cement porch floor and steps. The interior has oak floors in living room, dining room and hall; also panel wainscoting and beam ceilings. The rest of the house is finished with ordinary pine finish. The house is 36x38 and will cost about $4,000.

See floor plans next page.

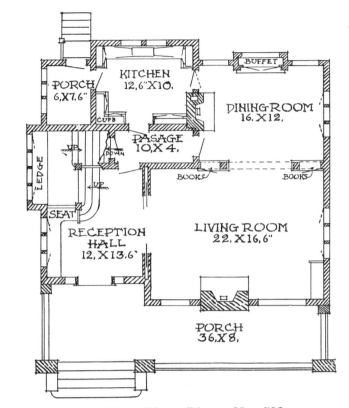

PORCH
6,X7.6"

KITCHEN
12,6"X10,

BUFFET

DINING ROOM
16,X12,

CUPB

PASAGE
10,X4,

BOOKS

BOOKS

LEDGE

UP

DOWN

UP

SEAT

RECEPTION
HALL
12,X13.6"

LIVING ROOM
22,X16,6"

PORCH
36,X8,

First Floor Plan. No. 533.

Complete plans and specifications of this house with all necessary interior details, either as shown on this page or reversed, will be furnished for $10.00.

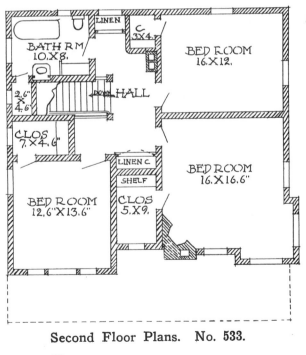

BATH RM
10,X8,

LINEN

C
3X4,

BED ROOM
16,X12,

2,6"
X
4,6"

DOWN HALL

CLOS
7,X4,6"

LINEN C

SHELF

BED ROOM
12,6"X13,6"

CLOS
5,X9,

BED ROOM
16,X16,6"

Second Floor Plans. No. 533.

No. 540.

Here we have a story and a half bungalow that is deservedly popular and which will find more builders as its merits become known. As we have already pointed out, there is at this time an increasing demand for this style of construction, and some new and original ideas are being brought out.

The cobblestone chimney and cobblestone foundation and pillars give the house an attractive individuality, while the large, roomy porch invites ease and comfort. The windows, with their small panes in the upper sashes revert somewhat to an old fashion, that harmonizes excellently well with the general plan. The front gable, finished in plaster, is a striking feature.

The interior shows a large living-room and reception hall with built-in bookcases in the buttresses. The reception hall and living-room are finished with hardwood floors and beam ceilings, and the dining-room is wainscoted with a heavy plate rail at the top.

The fireplace in the living-room shows a combination of cobblestone and Dutch clinker brick which produces a very desirable effect.

The fireplace has a wood shelf with brick brackets.

The breakfast-room can be used as a bed-room if desired. Upstairs there are three good-sized bed-rooms, bath-room, screen-room and balcony. The screen-room can be used as an open-air sleeping-room; indeed, the whole plan of construction lends itself well to diverse uses according to the needs or fancies of the occupants. Size over all, 32x49.

This house can be built for $3,500.

Complete plans and specifications of this house, with all necessary details, either as shown on this page or reversed, will be furnished for $10.00.

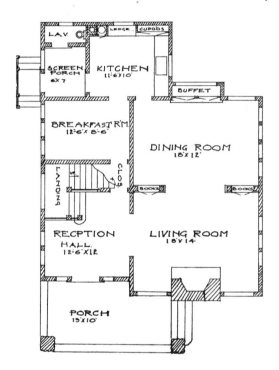

First Floor Plan. No. 540.

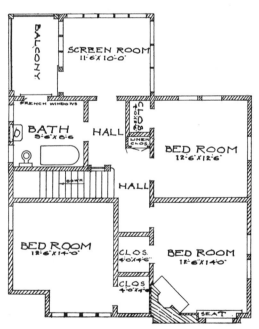

Second Floor Plan. No. 540.

71

No. 545.

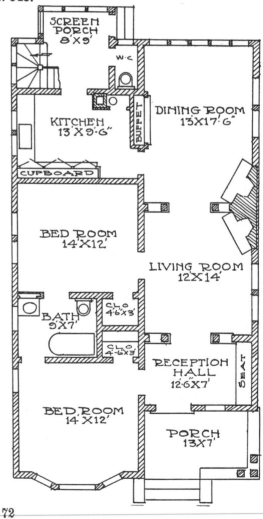

An inexpensive but attractive little bungalow is pictured on this page. The exterior is plain but attractive, while the interior is a model of convenience. The size of plan No. 545-A is 24x48 feet and can be built for about $1,250.

Complete plans and specifications of this house, with all necessary details, either as shown on this page or reversed, will be furnished for $10.00.

No. 554.

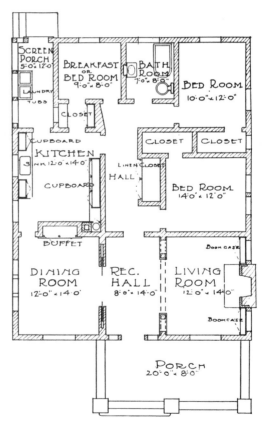

This six-room bungalow contains an amount of room often required by a small family needing only two or three sleeping-rooms. The inner hall, which may be lighted by glass upper panels in doors communicating with main hall and kitchen, occupies a central position, and a ready means of access to any room without passing through another room. The front part of the house can be thrown into a single room of ample size when required, and if preferred the columns and buttresses between the reception hall and living-room can be omitted, making the latter 14x20 feet in size. The exterior shows low pitched roofs with gable treatment, cobblestone porch and chimney, cement steps and porch floor, stained shingle walls, broad windows, and an air of quiet artistic refinement that is sure to appeal to good taste. Finished in pine, with oak floors, beam ceilings and paneled wainscot in the front rooms, the cost will be about $2,000.

Complete plans and specifications of this house, with all necessary details, either as shown on this page or reversed, will be furnished for $10.00.

73

No. 556.

This story-and-a-half nine room bungalow, 28x58 feet in size over all, is well suited to the needs of a family of liberal size. It has four bedrooms—two in the attic story, and a front roof balcony, which can be used as a sleeping porch; the breakfast room could also be used as an extra bedroom or as a sewing room. The cabinet kitchen with cupboards, drawers, bins and dwarf closets obviates the need of a separate pantry, and the three principal rooms, thrown into one by the open column and buttress treatment (with book cases in living room and den), gives a spacious appearance to the house upon entering that is very pleasing. Built with brick and cement porch, shingled walls and roof, oak floors, panelled wainscot and beamed ceilings in the three principal rooms, the cost will be about $2,500.

Complete plans and specifications of this house with all necessary interior details, either as shown on this page or reevrsed, will be furnished for $10.00.

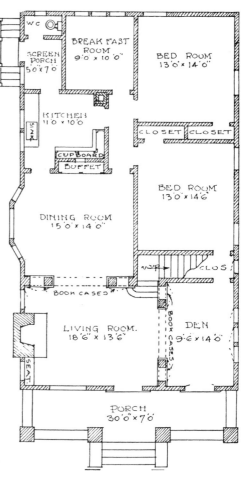

No. 565.

Here is another popular plan for a six-room bungalow with reception hall and rear hall. Note the large size of the rooms, and the convenience of arrangement. The cobblestone chimney in front also serves as a pillar, beyond which the wide bay window juts out attractively. Cobblestone is also used at the other end of the porch, in harmony with the general design. The exterior walls of this design are of red cedar shingles, with surfaced window and door trimmings.

This house can be built for $2,000. This bungalow is 42x49 over all.

Complete plans and specifications of this house, with all necessary details, either as shown on this page or reversed, will be furnished for $10.00.

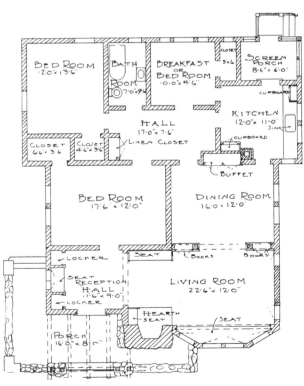

No. 567.

This is sure to prove a very popular plan with those who want comfort and snugness at a very moderate price, and at the same time have a home that will present on excellent appearance.

In addition to a good-sizd liv-ing-room, dining-room, two bed-rooms and a kitchen, there is a reception hall opening from the front porch, and a pergola in the rear.

The exterior is shingle, with a cobblestone pillar and diamond window in the living-room.

Some very pretty effects can be introduced in the staining and other colorings. Over all dimen-sion is 40x42.

The house can be built for $1,800.

Complete plans and specifica-tions of this house, with all neces-sary details, either as shown on this page or reversed, will be fur-nished for $10.00.

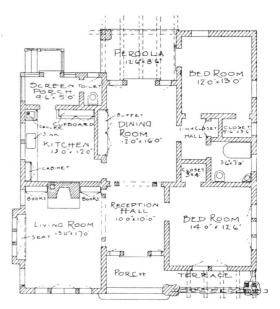

No. 572.

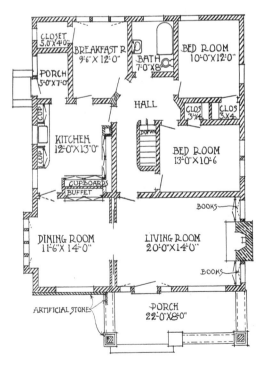

This handsome six-roomed bunga-low is very artistically set off by a stone front for the piazza, and stone pillars. The exterior is of cedar shingles with exterior trimmings of unsurfaced redwood. Interior, hard-wood floors, beam ceilings and pan-eled wainscoting.

The cost of this house is $2,000. The dimensions are 33x42.

Complete plans and specifications of this house, with all necessary de-tails, either as shown on this page or reversed, will be furnished for $10.00.

77

No. 573.

This bungalow possesses some odd features in the front gables which gives a very artistic effect and has been admired by many. The exterior is covered with shakes, with rough cast plaster to belt course. The chimney, front porch walls and piers are built of Dutch clinker brick, which also adds greatly to the artistic effect. The porch floors and steps are of cement. Living-room, dining-room and den have oak floors. The interior trim is slash grain pine; oak may be used if preferred. The den has a combination seat and wall bed, which makes a very desirable feature. Dining-room has an attractive buffet, and there is a well arranged cabinet kitchen. This bungalow is 34x54 feet and will cost about $2,250.

Complete plans and specifications of this house, with all necessary details, either as shown on this page or reversed, will be furnished for $10.00.

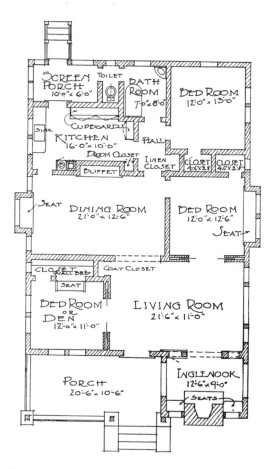

No. 574.

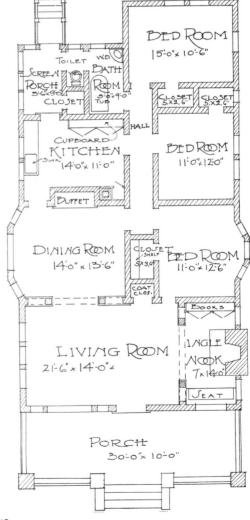

My attention was called, some years ago, to the disadvantage of posts being placed where the view was greatly obstructed and so to avoid this objection I originated the broad, unobstructed opening from corner to corner by supporting the roof upon a truss, a detail of which accompanied the plans.

In localities where boulders are available this design offers an excellent opportunity for their introduction; however, do not entertain an idea that boulders are entirely essential to the design, inasmuch as brick, cut stone or concrete may be used, producing an effect similar to that shown in the illustration.

Many are in love with the living-room extending across the front with the nook in one end, and judging from the number of sales of this design I am assured of its popularity. For a moderate priced home this is a real winner. Price complete, $2,500.

Complete plans and specifications of this house, with all necessary details, either as shown on this page or reversed, will be furnished for $10.00.

No. 576.

Here is a little gem that will appeal to every lover of inexpensive, artistic homes. Its irregular but harmonious lines will at once win a place in the heart of seekers for something pleasing.

This bungalow does not cost any more, but it "looks like more" and that is what most of us want, our money's worth; and for a comfortable, homelike bungalow to fit the ordinary purse it has few equals and no superiors. Cleverly arranged and indicative of ability in artistic designing this bungalow speaks for itself.

All of the conveniences of a larger and more pretentious home are embodied in this plan, and I delight in saying that many are the words of praise from those who are acquainted with and have used it for the construction of a home.

It has hardwood floors and panel wainscoting in living-room, dining-room and den. Built all complete will cost about $1,600. Dimensions, 30x43.

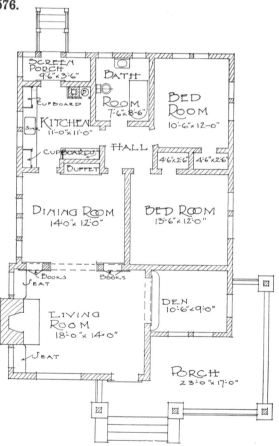

Complete plans and specifications of this house, with all necessary details, either as shown on this page or reversed, will be furnished for $10.00.

No. 578.

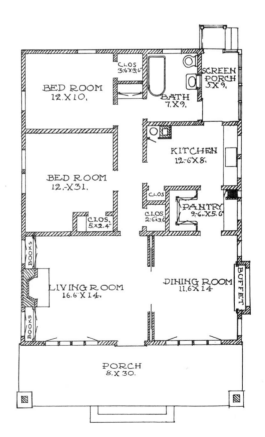

Here is a nice little bungalow of five rooms, inexpensive, but convenient and attractive. Note the wide, buttressed porch, and the size of the rooms. The plan includes a brick mantel with bookcase on either side, but there are no hardwood floors or beam ceilings. Dimensions over all, 30x47. The bungalow can be built for $1,200.

Complete plans and specifications of this house, with all necessary details, either as shown on this page or reversed, will be furnished for $10.00.

81

No. 580.

This bungalow is 28x46 feet inclusive of the porch.

The six rooms shown in the plan can be increased by finishing two rooms in the attic if desired, stairs leading from the hall making that plan perfectly feasible. Of course these rooms would not be full-height, except for a few feet at the center of the ceiling, but they would be very comfortable rooms nevertheless. Plainly but substantially built as shown the cost will be about $1,500.

Complete plans and specifications of this house, with all necessary details, either as shown on this page or reversed, will be furnished for $10.00.

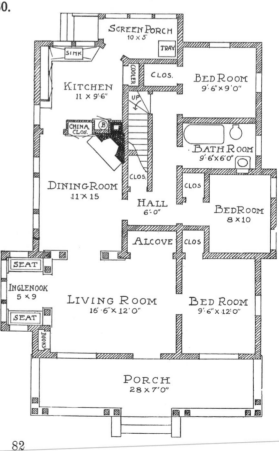

No. 581.

This extremely quaint bungalow will appeal only to those who like to have something distinctly "different." Living-room, dining-room and library have oak floors, panelled wainscot and beamed ceilings; and the first two have generous fireplaces also. Facing the entrance door of the living-room there is a console with large mirror which reflects the floor, ceiling and buttressed opening at the right hand, and incidentally the form of the visitor on entering. A stairway to the second floor leads from the small lobby behind the buffet, and rooms can be finished in the upper part of the house if needed in addition to the six rooms shown. This house should be placed upon a corner lot. If built with a north front, the terrace will be so shaded by the gable and library roof that the lack of a porch roof will not be very objectionable, and the bed-rooms will be light and sunny. The house as shown and described will cost about $2,000 to construct. The area of this house is 40x40.

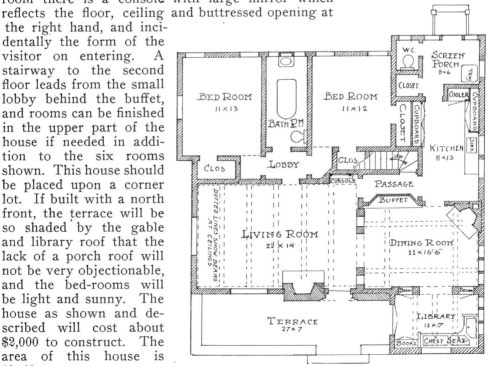

No. 582.

This bungalow, 30x43 feet 6 inches in size, contains all necessary accommodations for an ordinary family of moderate size and requirements, and is pleasing and dignified in appearance. It can be built for $1,600 to $1,750, depending upon the simplicity of finish; if beamed ceilings, etc., are desired, the larger amount will be required.

Complete plans and specifications of this house, with all necessary details, either as shown on this page or reversed, will be furnished for $10.00.

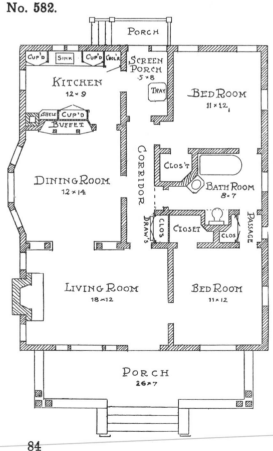

No. 583.

This is another of those "so different" bungalows that is certain to arrest the attention and arouse the curiosity of the prospective home builder, whenever seen.

Exterior walls as well as roof are covered with stained shingles, but sawed or split shakes having (or perhaps alternately 4 and 16) a weathering of about 16 inches can be substituted upon the walls at about the same cost.

The interior arrangement is clearly shown by the plan, and as will be seen is faultless. The living-room and dining-room have panelled wainscot and beamed ceilings, as well as hardwood floors; the kitchen and all the rear rooms are accessible from the interior hall and lobby, and somewhat unusual but desirable feature of a breakfast room is added, which if not desired can be used as an additional bed-room.

This bungalow covers a ground space of 32x46 feet and will cost about $1,800 to $2,000 according to inside finish.

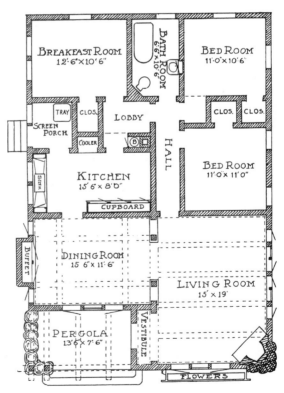

No. 606.

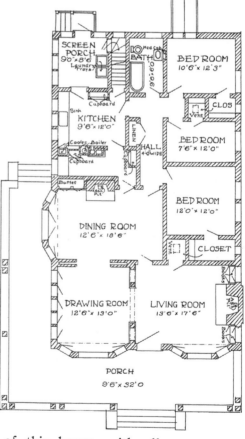

While the material and type of construction used are reminiscent of the English, yet this design is distinctly "Los Anglicized," by reason of its general proportions and internal arrangement. The exterior walls are brick veneered upon a wood frame, and carried to the ceiling joists, the gables being cement plaster enriched by half timber. The gables project slightly, forming an overhang that is supported on cove brackets, placed under each half timber carrying up a logical structural line.

The use of purlins to support the roof is more appropriate in this style than the local custom of bracket supports.

This design is admirably adapted to a corner lot, by reason of its gable treatment.

Living-room, dining-room and drawing-room have oak floors, beamed ceilings and panelled wainscoting. The dimensions are 30x50, not including porch. Cost to build, $2,300.

Complete plans and specifications of this house, with all necessary details, either as shown on this page or reversed, will be furnished for $10.00.

No. 623.

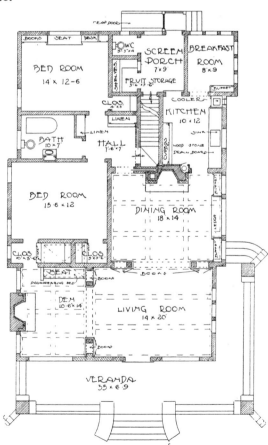

This bungalow is unique and classy. The exterior is of re-sawed siding. The porch walls and piers and step buttresses and the den chimney stack are built of rock-faced artificial stone, porch floor and steps are of cement. This bungalow has a cement floored cellar with space for furnace and a furnace flue running up in the dining-room chimney stack. There is also a large storage attic floored over and available for two or three bed-rooms if they should ever be desired; there is also a rear attic balcony. The living-room, dining-room and den are finished with slash grain pine, and have oak floors, beam ceilings and panelled wainscot. The bed-rooms, breakfast-room and bath are finished in white enamel. This measures 35x64 and will cost about $3,300 to build complete.

Plans and specifications, $10.00.

No. 627.

This design is a typical Wilson bungalow, including the characteristic and popular sweeping arch over the front porch. The buttresses appear to reinforce the porch piers and add an interesting line to the angles of the porch, which is built of ashlar jointed artificial stone. Resawed siding is specified for the weather-boarding.

The living-room, 14x22, is made attractive by a stone mantel and book cases on either side. Spaciousness is attained by the unbroken vista of the length of dining-room and living-room through the columned opening.

The use of chains as supports adds unusual interest in the treatment of the dining-room buffet. The screen sleeping-room, in connection with the rear bed-room, is well ventilated by reason of its corner location. More than ordinarily convenient is the breakfast-room and its relation to the surrounding rooms. It could be used as a den, if preferred.

Low wainscoting in the living-room and plate rail with plaster panels under are included in the estimated cost of $3,100. A fifty-foot lot would be required to give the space necessary for this bungalow. Two rooms could be finished in the attic.

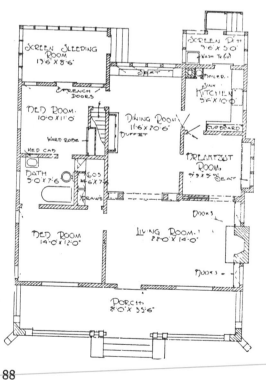

No. 629.

Number six hundred twenty-nine depends upon its proportions for a successful effect, rather than a superfluity of beams, flower boxes, etc. Artificial stone, used for the chimneys and porch, give it a substantial appearance. An unrestricted view and breadth of effect are produced by the wide arch which is trussed over. Resawed siding is specified for the weather-boarding.

Leaded glass doors in the book cases, alongside of the brick mantel, serving ledge and built-in buffet, all tend to the beauty of the home. The buffet kitchen is well arranged with cupboards and drawers. There can be two or three rooms finished on second floor if desired. This bungalow is 30x53, and will cost to build about $2,500.

Complete plans and specifications of this house, with all necessary details, either as shown on this page or reversed, will be furnished for $10.00.

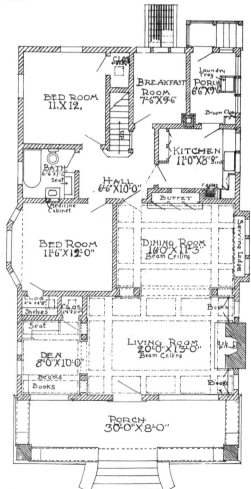

No. 632.

A very pleasing bungalow is shown in this view. Cobblestones and clinker brick are used with good result for porch and chimney.

The principal and subordinate gable scheme is introduced with an effect that is gratifying to the appreciative bungalow connoiseur.

Shingles are used for the gable walls. Resawed siding covers the main walls of the exterior. This view does not convey any adequate impression of the beauty of the other side of this bungalow, with its terrace, pergola, and gabled bay window.

The interior arrangement is good.

The breakfast room is located close to the kitchen and could be adapted to use as a screen sleeping-room.

The estimated cost of this bungalow is $1,900. Its total dimensions, exclusive of porches, 28½x48 feet.

Complete plans and specifications of this house, with all necessary details, either as shown on this page or reversed, will be furnished for $10.00.

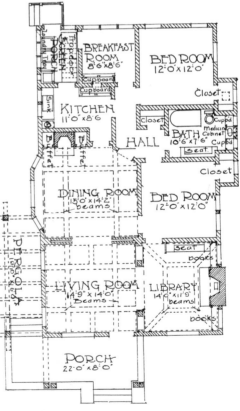

No. 537.

The dining-room windows are grouped into one bay, forming a space in which a seat is built. The buffet and fire-place are united into one design. The brick fire-place has a heavy wood mantel shelf, supported on cove brackets. Commendable judgment is shown in placing bedrooms on the corners of a plan—there being not only more satisfactory ventilation, but also increases the possibility of obtaining the benefits of sunshine, which greatly enhances the value of a bed-room, from the view of hygienics.

The kitchen is small, but would meet the requirements of a family of the size that would occupy this house. Located as it is, the fireplace would assist in the desired economy by concentrating the kitchen flue and mantel flue into one chimney.

This bungalow is 28x45, and could be built for $1,350.

Complete plans and specifications of this house, with all necessary details, either as shown on this page or reversed, will be furnished for $10.00.

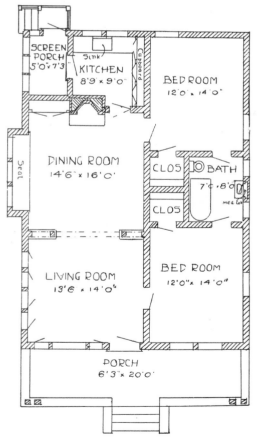

No. 635.

No. 635 is more pleasing, architecturally, than many bungalows of its size. The gabled entrance porch is generally associated with plans that meet the popular favor.

Resawed siding is specified on the exterior walls, shingles as indicated form the covering for the walls of the dormers.

Straight lines have been used with good judgment in the disposition of the wood bars, which subdivide the glass of the windows.

The serving ledge in the dining-room is built in a small bay window, which adds a great deal to the pleasing exterior. As will be noted on the accompanying floor plans, the fireplace is located in the dining-room instead of being built in the living-room as is customary.

This arrangement may be changed if desired.

Beam ceiling and wood wainscoting are included in both the living-room and dining-room.

Sliding doors separate the living-room from the den and dining-room.

Between the living-room and the staircase hall is an opening, cased the same height as the doors and windows, and supported by chamfered columns on buttresses that are a continuation of the wainscot.

A little re-arranging of this plan would entitle the builder to make cellar stairway, descending under the stairway to the second floor; an outside entrance at the grade could probably be effected at this point if desirable. Under the present plan the laundry work could be done on the screen porch.

The kitchen is amply supplied with cupboards; drawers and paneled doors are built under the drain-boards of the sink.

The stairway to the upper floor lands in a hallway, well lighted and ventilated by the window on the landing of the stairway.

Large closets are included for the two bed-rooms, small windows giving light and ventilation to the closets.

Casement windows are shown and specified on the plans of this bungalow.

The front porch projects seven feet beyond the line of the main house, which is 28x35 feet.

To build it as shown with beamed ceilings and wainscoting in the living-room and dining-room would cost $2,500.

Complete plans and specifications of this house, with all necessary details, either as shown on this page or reversed, will be furnished for $10.00.

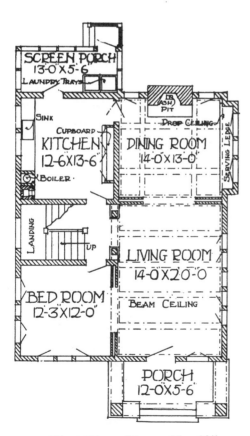

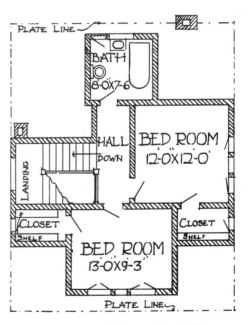

First Floor Plan.   No. 635.   Second Floor Plan.   No. 635.

No. 636.

This design presents, in composite form, the satisfactory features of a house with side gables and one with "fore and aft" gables. The overhanging second story in the side gables is as beneficial to the outside appearance as it is useful in enlarging the bed-rooms above.

The exterior walls of the first story are covered with resawed siding above and plaster below the floor level. Shingles form the gables. Artificial stone is used for the chimneys and porch, which has cement floor and steps. The use of purlins to support the wide overhang of roof is in harmony with the generous breadth of this bungalow.

The wide arch, first conceived in the Wilson bungalow, is a feature which is used whenever appropriate because of the resulting unity and the unobstructed view. The study given to this design is evident in the disposition of the different parts, externally and internally.

Originality is displayed in the handling of the brick mantel, book cases, and ceiling beams in the living-room.

The sliding doors, between living-room and den, would isolate the latter, if desired, when in use as a "smokery." The dining-room, which is very spacious, is provided with beamed ceiling, large bay window and a buffet possessed of original features.

A built-in buffet is also included in the convenient breakfast room. Generous cupboards, flower bins and drainboards are kitchen features.

On the screen porch is a toilet in addition to the bath-room, which is well located between the two bed-rooms, making a complete seven-room house on the ground floor, without the two bed-rooms and a screen sleeping-room above, which are included in the estimated cost of $3,500.

A stairway on the screen porch leads to the basement, the walls of which are concrete. It is floored with cement and provided with a flue that would admit of its being used as a furnace room or laundry. This plan is 32x59, not including front porch.

Complete plans and specifications of this house, with all necessary details, either as shown on this page or reversed, will be furnished for $10.00.

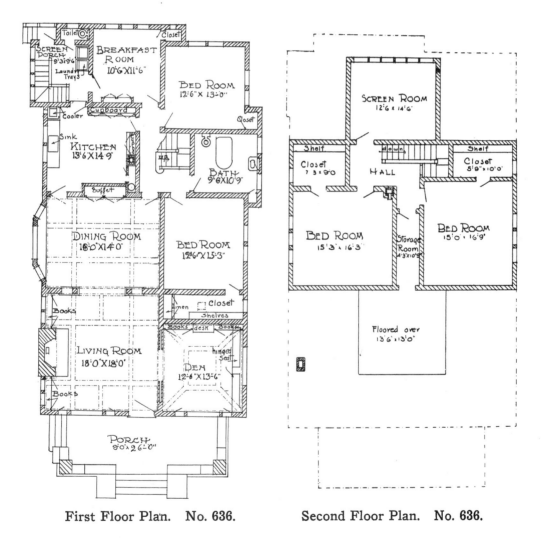

First Floor Plan.   No. 636.   Second Floor Plan.   No. 636.

No. 640.

Breadth and simplicity form the basis for the winning qualities of No. 640, which could be built very successfully on a 50-foot lot, despite its apparent requirement of a greater area for its building site. It is broad, yet built economically, the front porch and steps being wood, instead of cement. Shingles form the covering for both the roof and the side walls and gables.

The bolster caps of the double porch columns are treated effectively by the manner in which their ends are sawed. The ridge board is wood. Purlins piercing the verge boards support the roof. A group of beveled plate glasses enrich the front door.

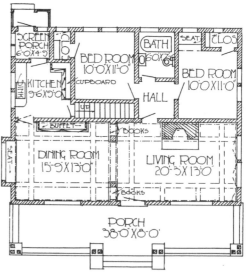

Living and dining-room, being separated merely by the columns shown in the accompanying illustration, are practically one room, divided by buttresses which have built-in bookcases on either side; these two rooms have beam ceilings, panel wainscoting and oak floors. This plan is 38x36 and will cost $1,750.

Complete plans and specifications of this house, with all necessary details, either as shown on this page or reversed, will be furnished for $10.00.

No. 641.

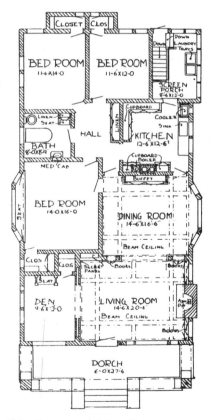

This bungalow has the same broad span over the front porch that is the striking feature of No. 443, though there is quite a distinct difference in the details of the porch timber work and the other parts of the exterior. Artificial stone is used for the masonry of the porch and chimneys. Sliding doors are indicated between the den and living-room, which, with the dining-room, has a beam ceiling.

The buffet is an unusually good design, including a punch-bowl receptacle and doors below the counter shelf, having opalescent glass panels.

The width is 32, length 64 feet. Estimated cost is $2,800.

Complete plans and specifications of this house, with all necessary details, either as shown on this page or reversed, will be furnished for $10.00.

No. 651.

A type of stucco bungalow is shown here. Much of the details and general appearance of bungalows of this class are inspired by the Spanish, colonial or mission style. This class of construction is becoming very popular. Metal tile was specified on the roof of this bungalow, and harmonizes well with the style, though the original Spanish tile are more in keeping with this subject.

If well executed, a stucco finish leaves nothing to be desired as to durability, color and texture. There are several different ways of manipulating the application of the exterior plaster to secure artistic variations in the surface of the walls. Stippling the wet plaster—applying the stiff bristles of a brush against the wall, the employment of the "pebble dash" or "paddle dash" impart crisp effects that makes plastered fully as satisfactory, artistically, as the result when using other materials that are more expensive.

The living room of No. 651 contains a pressed brick mantel. A wood cornice occurring at the juncture of the side walls and ceiling forms a simple and inexpensive treatment of the ceilings of the dining-room and living-room. The small entrance porch makes it possible to use the pergola as a living-porch in connection with the dining-room. The dimensions of this house are 29x36 feet, and will cost about $1,500 to build.

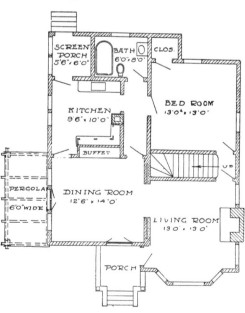

No. 656.

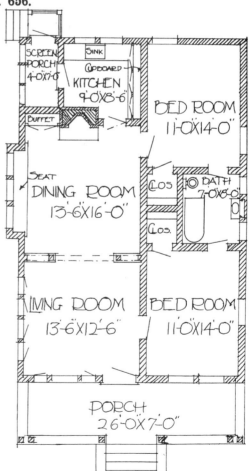

Compactness of plan and simplicity of design were the objects desired in planning this inexpensive bungalow. It is built with resawed siding for the weather-boarding and a shingle roof.

A belt course at the main window sills carries out the broad bungalow lines.

The internal arrangement could not be made more economical in size, as all space is utilized. A commendable and noteworthy feature is the corner location of the bedrooms and the living room—a merit that is often sacrificed in larger homes.

The opening between the living room and dining room extends to the same height as the doors and windows and is cased the same; buttresses, at the customary height for wainscoting, form the bases of the short tapering columns which support the arch.

The main width of this plain is 26 feet, beyond which the bay window projects 1½ feet; the length is 45 feet, including the seven-foot front porch; $1,475 is the estimated cost of constructing No. 547.

Complete plans and specifications, $10.00.

99

No. 657.

In the gabled entrance porch may be found an explanation of the charm of this bungalow. Shingles are used in this gable, and with the unique mode of ventilation contribute materially to the satisfactory appearance of the exterior, which is covered with resawed siding. Split stone is specified laid in irregular ashlar jointing.

This illustration gives an impression of the appearance of a California bungalow in Eastern surroundings. Many persons who have viewed a subject of this kind amid the semi-tropical surroundings of Southern California have formed an opinion that such a setting is necessary for the success of a California bungalow.

This is a misconception and an underestimation of the cosmopolitan nature of this form of residence, which is based upon simplicity and logical construction—qualities that are never outgrown or become inappropriate. For this reason the bungalow is equally at home among date palms and banana trees or under sheltering branches of maple or oak.

The widely projecting roof of this bungalow would lose none of its inviting appearance, even though it may be covered with snow.

Considerable originality is noticeable in the posts and balustrade of the porch. In this view, one may see only a small portion of the roof of the screen sleeping-room, which is an important part of the rear elevation and second floor plan.

Wood bars divide the glass of the windows, which are of the type hung on weights, sliding up and down.

An unusual feature of this plan is the presence of a reception hall, separated from the dining-room by sliding doors. Instead of the usual location, in the living-room, the fireplace has been placed in the dining-room; it is built of pressed brick.

The buffet is of generous width and, with the china closet and seat, occupies one entire side wall of the dining-room.

The unusual location of the mantel has resulted in one economy, being situated so that the kitchen flue and fireplace flue are carried up in one chimney.

One entire side of the living-room is devoted to a built-in seat, the central portion of which is provided with a hinged lid; at either side are book-cases composed of open shelves, underneath which are drawers.

Ceiling beams are included in the dining-room.

In each of the two bed-rooms, lavatories have been built; this may be omitted if preferred, the additional space being thrown into closet room.

A stairway to the basement leads from the screen porch, while on the second floor is a fine large screen room reached from the hall stairway. The total dimensions of the house are 32x40 feet, exclusive of porches, etc. It would cost $2,000.

Complete plans and specifications of this house, with all necessary details, either as shown on this page or reversed, will be furnished for $10.00.

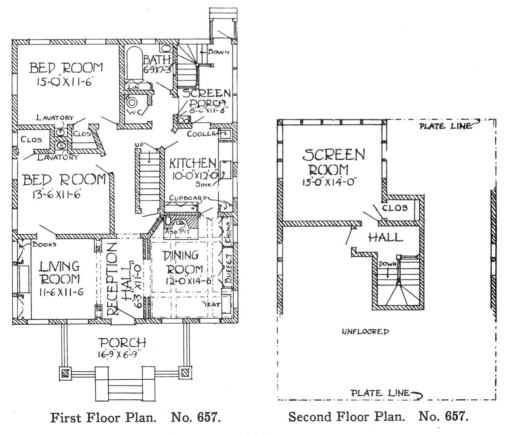

First Floor Plan.   No. 657.   Second Floor Plan.   No. 657.

No. 658R.

The suffixed "R" indicates that this design is the reverse of the original plan; it might not be inappropriate to call the reader's attention to the fact that any design shown in the Bungalow Book can be furnished reversed— identically the same in every respect as the original plans would appear on transparent paper, viewed from the back excepting that the figures and letters are not backward on either the original or reversed plans. This offer applies to all of our stock plans, which we furnish either in the original form or reversed at the price of Ten Dollars.

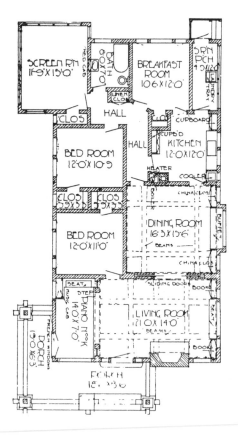

No. 658R is one of the most pleasing bungalows that has recently been built from our plans. The exterior is composed of cobblestone clinker brick and shakes covered with asbestos roofing and batten strips.

The interior is finished in modern bungalow finish. The estimated cost is $2,500.

Complete plans and specifications of this house, with all necessary details, either as shown on this page or reversed, will be furnished for $10.00.

No. 661.

This attractive bungalow shows some of the characteristics of the Swiss chalet, notably in the pierced vertical boards used on the balconies. The wide projection of the roof and the open arch in the front gable contributes materially to the Swiss appearance.

The living-room is a broad conception, extending from the front to the rear of the house, French doors being included besides the other windows.

The mantel is built of sandstone. The pass pantry between the dining-room and kitchen may be omitted if desired.

A flight of steps at this point forms the combination stairway that gives all of the advantage of a separate rear stairway.

The plan covers an area 45x54 feet, total dimensions. It could be built at a cost of $2,550.

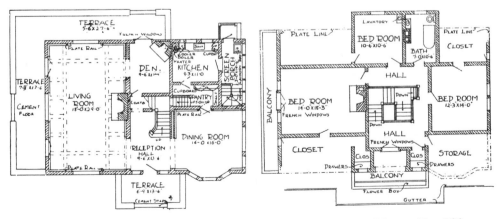

First Floor Plan.   No. 661.   Second Floor Plan.   No. 661.

103

No. 676.

The first glimpse of this house arouses the interest and admiration of all lovers of the beautiful and appropriate in domestic architecture.

Asbestos roofing permits the creation in this instance of a very pleasing arrangement of the broken roof lines. A wood ridge defines the lines of the snowy white asbestos. Resawed siding below the belt course, forms the base of the house, battering out in graceful profile and forming a variation in texture when contrasted with the shakes above, laid in alternate narrow and wide courses.

The continuous head-casing of the doors and windows projects at the corners, making a uniquely artistic accent of the construction.

Projecting purlins support the widely overhanging roof.

Plaster is used for the porch, columns and chimney.

The interior is by no means lacking in the individuality that marks the exterior. Entering the living room, the attention is called to the mantel, an original creation in which plaster and clinker brick play the leading part.

A chimney breast of the same material is carried up in lesser width to the ceiling, a wood shelf forming the place where this deviation occurs. The arrangement of ceiling beams is good. In placing sliding doors between living-room and dining-room the builder has recognized the desire of many who wish to have a means of separating these rooms.

Sliding doors also are used between the front bed-room and the living-room.

The upper part of the buffet in the dining-room is bay shaped, supported on a small beam which is suspended by chains attached to the wall, just above the wainscot, which continues over the shelf of the buffet instead of the customary mirror.

An open archway occurs between the dining-room and breakfast room. The latter is also in close relation to the pergola. The ceiling of the breakfast-room is broken into squares by 3-inch battens, forming a very successful background upon which to fresco, in delicate tints, a grape vine, the fruit and foliage of which are seen as through a trellis formed by the ceiling battens. This design may be made to continue down the side walls if desired.

In a room of comparatively small dimensions any treatment in the way of wall or ceiling decorations should be kept in delicate tones to avoid the effect of apparently reducing the size of the room.

The pergola, which is visible from either the breakfast-room or the dining-room, through the French doors, serves the purpose of admitting light into the dining-oom.

An opportunity to create a very artistic feature of the pergola porch is made possible by the pool constructed of cement in which fish and aquatic

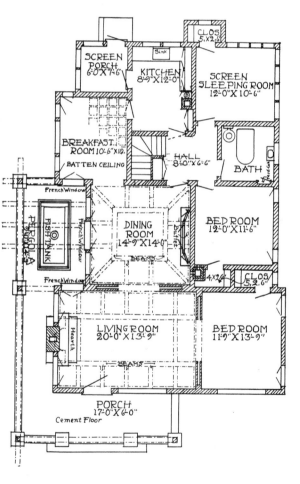

plants would make a very pleasing addition to the home, in the opinion of many nature lovers.

In the kitchen an unusual addition to the compact cupboard plan, is present in the form of an ironing board, hinged at the larger end with a rod under, folding up against the cupboard when not in use.

A brick flue was not included, being designed for the use of a gas range. The bath-room is well located between the screen sleeping-room and second bed-room.

A flue is located in the second bed-room, with terra cotta thimbles into that room and the dining-room.

Altogether, No. 676 is a home that gives proof of more than average taste on the part of its owner.

Built complete, this house will cost about $2,700.

Complete plans and specifications of this house, with all necessary details, either as shown on this page or reversed, will be furnished for $10.00.

No. 688.

The irregular courses of rubble stone is admirably adapted to the rugged simplicity of the California bungalow. Japanese flower pots are well proportioned to suitably terminate the heavy central piers of the porch.

Observe the satisfying result of the manner in which the corner piers are built, giving strength on the corner and preserving a feeling of unity in connection with the smaller isolated piers, which receive the porch balustrade.

This plan is well adapted to a corner lot, by reason of external design and interior arrangement. The chimney, bay window and two gables occur on the same side of the house as does the living and dining rooms. Resawed siding is specified for the weatherboarding. The interior is well finished. The size of the house is 28x52 and will cost about $2,000.

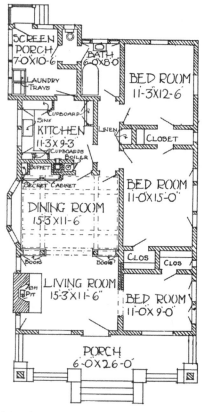

Complete plans and specifications of this house, with all necessary details, either as shown on this page or reversed, will be furnished for $10.00.

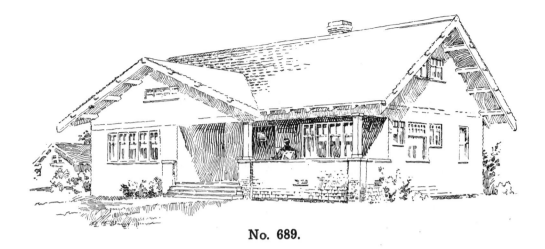

No. 689.

A commodious bungalow, 40x36 feet in dimensions, containing five rooms below and two in the roof.

There is cement-floored basement under a portion of the house, and brick or concrete foundations for the whole.

Living and dining rooms have oak floors, plaster-paneled wainscot and beamed ceilings.

Living-room has brick mantel, bookcases and seat, and dining-room has recessed buffet.

Stairs lead to chamber and to basement. The cost of this bungalow is about $2,500.

Complete plans and specifications of this house, with all necessary details, either as shown on this page or reversed, will be furnished for $10.00.

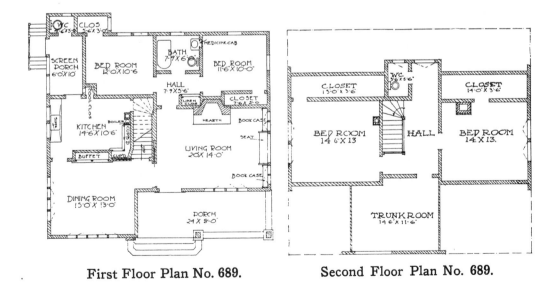

First Floor Plan No. 689.   Second Floor Plan No. 689.

No. 690.

The above title is based on the assumption that the one large room, extending across the entire front, is really two rooms.

This is a full two-story house, but has the architectural features that has made the Wilson bungalow famous.

The porch and open balcony to the right are counterbalanced by the brick chimney to the left. The timber continuing around the house unites the windows and overcomes all the disagreeable stilted appearance that is so frequently produced in a two-story house designed upon bungalow lines. The porch being only partly across the front secures for the living room a generous supply of light.

The stairway is located conveniently in the center of the house, and is provided with a combination kitchen and living-room entrance to the landing, from which one flight leads to the second floor.

The living-room mantel is six feet wide, built of pressed brick, which corbels out to support the wood shelf.

A feature with which some housekeepers may prefer to dispense is the pantry on the rear screen porch. The kitchen is of sufficient length to admit the introduction of additional cupboards, if required.

The toilet may be entered separately from the bath-room. The bed-room on the first floor is in connection with a large ventilated closet.

If it be desired to square the hall and front bed-room on the second floor, this result could be attained by the incorporating of a sewing-room in the space occupied by the boudoir.

This would make the corner bed-room 14x10 feet, with a very large ventilated closet between this and the adjoining bed-room. A hall linen closet could be successfully cut off one end of this closet and still leave ample closet space for the front bed-room.

The open balcony is of sufficient size to be used for an outdoor sleeping-room.

The first floor of this house is 29¾ feet wide; the length is 41¼ feet, including the 7½ foot projection of the front porch. The estimated cost is $2,250.

Complete plans and specifications of this house, with all necessary details, either as shown on this page or reversed, will be furnished for $10.00.

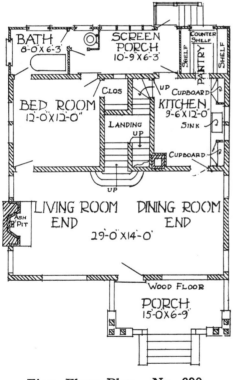

First Floor Plan. No. 690.

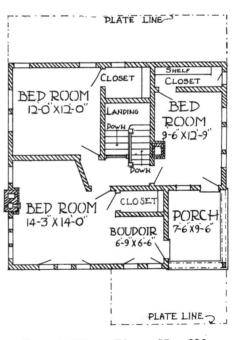

Second Floor Plan. No. 690.

No. 693.

An unsymmetrical but pleasing elevation is presented by No. 693. The small gable seems to have been designed as a shelter for the vine which has grown up under the eaves. There is considerable individuality in the manner in which the porch timbers are cut.

Resawed siding is specified on all parts of the exterior walls. The brackets which support the roofs are composed of two straight members, and the brace, which has two coves.

The bay window, which is a very acceptable relief to the plain side shown here, is roofed with asbestos, as is also the main house.

The library, living-room and dining-room have oak floors, panel wainscot and beam ceilings. However, these may be omitted if so desired. Estimated cost is $1,850.

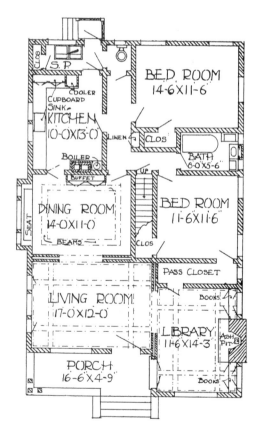

Complete plans and specifications of this house, with all necessary details, either as shown on this page or reversed, will be furnished for $10.00.

110

No. 706.

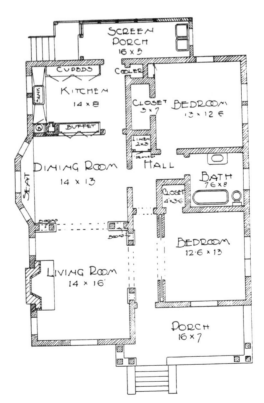

This 32x40 bungalow (exclusive of screen porch) contains five rooms of generous size and of commodious arrangement.

The exterior of the bungalow is constructed of studding covered with resawed redwood siding for walls, and shingled gables stained two coats of any desired color,—brown or green will look well,—with roof of a lighter color,—white or silver gray will harmonize with the stained work and the painted trimmings, which may be either white or cream-color.

The front steps and buttresses are of cement and the porch floor of wood, slightly pitched to the steps and scupper.

This bungalow can be built for $1,500.

Complete plans and specifications of this house, with all necessary details, either as shown on this page or reversed, will be furnished for $10.00.

No. 707.

This 28x33 foot four-room bungalow is compact, simple and unpretentious; just the thing for a small family that does not entertain much company nor care for an elaborate style of living.

The kitchen, the rear bed-room and bath-room are accesible from the hall, which opens out of the living-room and which contains a case of three drawers with a small linen closet over.

Built and finished in an inexpensive manner, this bungalow may be completed for about $850 to $1,000.

Complete plans and specifications of this house, with all necessary details, either as shown on this page or reversed, will be furnished for $10.00.

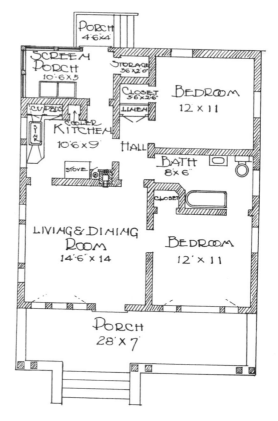

112

No. 708:

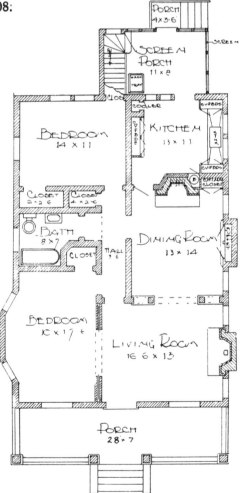

A five-room bungalow 28x47 feet exclusive of screen porch, with attic space for storage, or two bed-rooms may be finished off in the front and rear, leaving the central part for storage. The attic is accessible from the screen porch by a rather steep run of stairs.

The living-room and dining-room are en-suite, being separated only by a pillar and buttress opening, and have handsome fireplaces, a buffet, and a china closet with leaded glass doors, drawers, etc. The front bed-room can also be thrown into the same suite by running the sliding doors into their pockets, giving about 600 square feet of floor area in practically one room for social emergencies.

This bungalow can be built for $1,650 to $1,800—possibly somewhat less if built with a strict regard to economy of construction and finish.

Complete plans and specifications of this house, with all necessary details, either as shown on this page or reversed, will be furnished for $10.00.

No. 711.

We present here something of a novelty—Bungalow Real Estate Office, suitable for a city or suburban location anywhere,—East, West, North or South. There is no doubt whatever that such an office will, in a short time, pay for itself in the extra amount of business it will attract, and the class of people that will naturally gravitate to it by very reason of its novelty and its quiet air of respectability and "tone." Such an office as is here pictured would at once banish all feeling of distrust and uncertainty from the mind of an investor, and thus clear the way at once for a profitable business negotiation, and in this way, if in no other, "it would pay."

The Real Estate agent is a useful as well as a respected man in any community, and should surround himself with an environment suggestive of that usefulness, and conducive to confidence upon the part of the best elements of his city or town.

It is his legitimate business to find a customer for the man or woman wishing to sell or rent property, and to secure for the home-seeker or other investor such house, lot or land as he may desire; and his ability to do so is a full and complete vindication for his profession or business; a business that may be made highly remunerative in almost any town or community if conducted upon honorable business principles.

A profitable Real Estate business is built up frequently from very modest beginnings; therefore we have planned this building in such a way as to make it available for an expanding business, by arranging two small rear rooms so that one or both may be rented to other parties, with or without desk-room in the General Office, a side entrance door furnishing access in the latter case.

Both entrance doors are emphasized by roof canopies supported by brackets, and the rear door is approached from the front under a vine-embowered pergola. If the approach is from a side street, it may be screened from the front by a vine-covered lattice work between the rear pergola post and the building.

The largest of these rear rooms may be warmed with an air-tight stove discharging the smoke into one of the two flues of the chimney shown, the other serving for the fireplace of the general office.

Whenever the volume of business transacted came to warrant the expansion, the small rear office could be withdrawn from rental and taken for use—still renting out the larger office until that too became a necessity. The partition between the two front offices could then be removed leaving only a broad cased opening,—the general office extending across the entire front, and one of the rear rooms being used as the private office.

The plan calls for a building 22x24 feet in size, with a low-pitched asbestos "ready-roofing" roof, secured with painted wooden battens, and a pressed brick chimney with cement housing over flues. The exterior shows mission timbering effects in corner posts, joists, sills and casings, and picturesque door canopies and pergola of undressed timbers. The walls are covered with sawed shakes or may be shingles and simply oiled two or three coats, forming an agreeable contrast with the stained timbers and the painted window sash and sill. This office building will cost about $500.

Complete plans and specifications of this house, with all necessary details, either as shown on this page or reversed, will be furnished for $10.00.

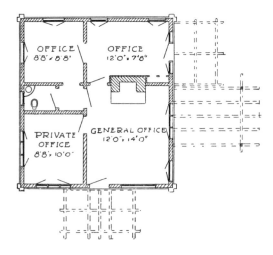

No. 716.

This is a handsome and commodious mission style residence. The exterior walls are of trowled cement plaster in stipple finish, laid upon galvanized expanded metal lath, over heavily sheathed walls of frame construction, and have cement balcony copings.

The low-pitched and heavily projecting roofs and the chimney-caps are of Mission pattern red terra-cotta tiles, with lap-joint hip and ridge-rolls and finals. The main deck-roof is covered with "Rubberoid Roofing," and the balcony floor with painted canvas.

This residence is 44 by 53 feet in size, and has seven rooms below and five above, in addition to a large staircase hall in the second story.

There is a cement basement underneath the entire house, accessible through an outside rear door and by stairs from the kitchen, containing a laundry, a furnace room, a toilet and a large storage area.

The first story consists of an entrance hall with handsome open string stairs to second story, and is entered through a four-foot door from the porch. Upon the left hand is the living-room, 14x21 feet in dimensions, separated from the hall mainly by a 12-foot 6-inch cased opening with two octagonal wood columns, these rooms thus being thrown into one. At the rear of the entrance hall there is a large inner court, 24 feet in length by 13 in width, with a tessellated cement tile floor, from the center of which rises a massive water basin, with low but handsomely moulded elliptic curb about one and one-half feet high and nearly 14 feet in length.

A bronzed fountain consisting of two shallow circular basins of Roman design and of graceful proportions rise from the center of this basin, the lower and larger of which is about 3 feet 8 inches in diameter, and the other about 2 feet, with a rim five feet above the floor of the court.

This house built complete with hardwood floors and trim on first floor, and equipped with hot water heating plant will cost about $10,000.

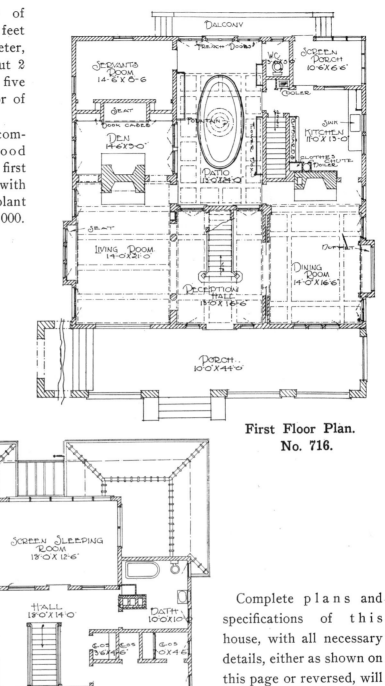

First Floor Plan.
No. 716.

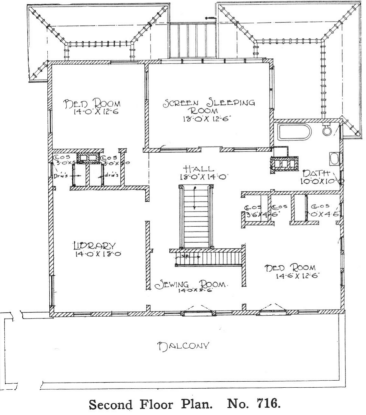

Complete plans and specifications of this house, with all necessary details, either as shown on this page or reversed, will be furnished for $10.

Second Floor Plan.   No. 716.

No. 717.

It would be hard to find a more pleasing design for a small bungalow than is here presented. The charm of it consists largely in its massive simplicity and the artistic balance of proportions. Notice the unusually heavy barge boards and porch posts — twelve inches and fourteen inches, respectively — and the extremely low roofs — not more than "one-fifth pitch," to use a carpenter's vernacular description.

The porch piers and chimney are of dark red bricks, the steps and porch floor of cement, and the exterior walls and roof of shingles, oiled and allowed to weather, or stained, as owner may prefer.

The finish of the interior is of pine, using slash-grain for the principal rooms, and plain-sawed for the balance. Oak floors in the two principal rooms and pine elsewhere.

Plaster paneled wainscot and beamed ceilings in the two principal rooms, all others to be plastered down to the baseboards.

This bungalow is 33x44 feet in size, exclusive of porch, and will cost about $2,000.

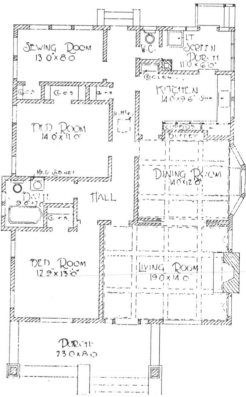

No. 718.

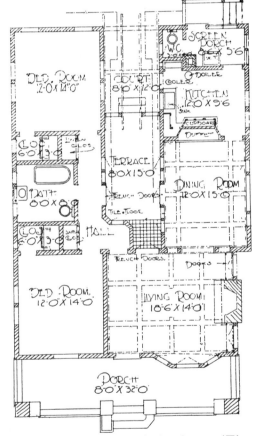

Here is another bungalow whose every line shows a high degree of artistic merit, and the plan is nearly ideal in all that counts for beauty, comfort and convenience. It is 32 feet long at the front and 34 at the rear, and is 54 feet deep, including the porch.

While there are only five rooms, not counting bath-room, screen porch and interior hall, the plan is such that the terrace in the rear court — communicating as it does with all the principal rooms of the house — forms an open air room. It is entirely screened from outside observation by the two rear wings and by the vines trained over the pergola at the rear end of the court, and is used as an out-of-door dining-room, sitting-room and sleeping-room combined.

The porch floor and steps are of cement, and the porch walls, piers and balustrades of cement and artificial stones in two colors as shown. The walls and roof are shingled and stained, and barge boards, rafter ends, brackets and porch entablature are of stained rough lumber. (The awning shown is arranged to extend forward over four wrought iron brackets, forming a canopy over the central part of the porch.)

This bungalow will cost from $2,400 to $2,600, depending upon the finish, etc.

119

No. 719.

In this design the use of Asbestos Roofing has made possible a very pleasing effect of lowness without sacrificing the necessary height for a light living-room and roof ventilation, very essential in this type of a house, which is well adapted for a corner lot.

The successful exterior is due to the admirable handling of the roof lines—a practical demonstration of the fallacy of the belief that an artistic bungalow depends upon elaborate details and expensive masonry. Note the unity of effect produced in the windows by the lintel-like head casings, accentuated by the absence of side casings,—possible with casement windows. Shakes are used for the exterior walls.

Where shakes are not available, shingles may be used instead. The interior has all modern conveniences. This bungalow is 30x57 feet and will cost about $1,900.

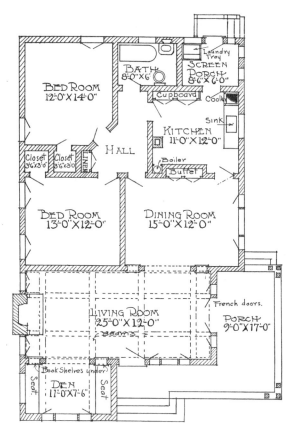

Complete plans and specifications of this house, with all necessary details, either as shown on this page or reversed, will be furnished for $10.00.

No. 457.

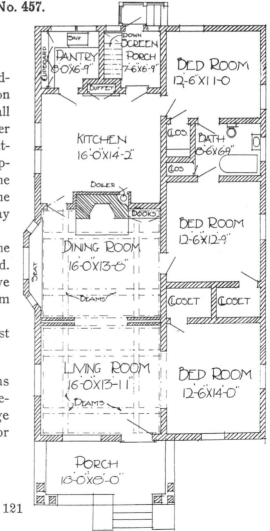

No. 457. A very satisfactory handling of the front porch proposition is evident in the selection of the small gable with its ventilators and flower box. Purlins supporting the projecting roofs add materially to the appearance of the front elevation. The requisite diversity is secured for the side elevation by the living room bay window and the chimney.

Resawed siding is specified for the walls. The interior is well finished. The living room and dining room have oak floors, panel wainscoting and beam ceilings.

The house is 30x52 and will cost about $200.00.

Complete plans and specifications of this house, with all necessary details, either as shown on this page or reversed, will be furnished for $10.00.

121

No. 720.

In this design simplicity is obtained by the use of only two materials in the exterior walls—plaster for the porch piers, chimneys and base, with shingles above and on the roofs.

The front bed-room may be used as a den or library in connection with the living-room, which has a brick mantel, low wainscot and beam ceiling, like No. 719.

Beam ceilings, panels, wainscot, plate rail and buffet, contribute to the desirable qualities of the dining-room. The kitchen is arranged for convenience. The most notable feature of this plan is the large screen room, which by means of the French doors, may be used in connection with rear bed-room as a sleeping-room or furnished with a separate bed. The large closet would be useful for this purpose or in case of the screen-room being used as a "gymnasium—nursery"; it is admirably adapted to this or use as a conservatory. Glass could be substituted for the screens, in eastern climates, if desired, in the winter. The toilet is conveniently located.

Large, ventilated closets are provided for all bed-rooms on both floors. The linen closet is a capacious and useful feature.

A conveniently located inside, cellar stairway is built under the main stairway.

This design covers 36x52 feet. To build it complete with hardwood floors and beamed ceilings in the living and dining-rooms, pine finish elsewhere, would cost approximately $3,300.

See floor plans on next page.

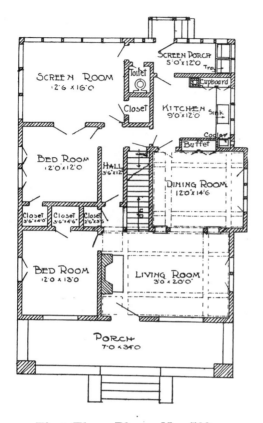

SCREEN ROOM
12'6 x 16'0

SCREEN PORCH
5'0 x 12'0 Tray

Toilet

Cupboard

Closet

KITCHEN
9'0 x 12'0 Sink

BED ROOM
12'0 x 12'0

HALL
3'6 x 12

Cooler
Buffet

DINING ROOM
12'0 x 14'6

Closet
3'6 x 4'0

Closet
3'6 x 4'6

Closet
2'6 x 3'6

BED ROOM
12'0 x 13'0

LIVING ROOM
13'0 x 20'0

PORCH
7'0 x 34'0

First Floor Plan.   No. 720.

Complete plans and specifications of this house, with all necessary details, either as shown on this page or reversed, will be furnished for $10.

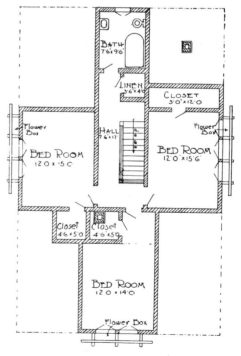

BATH
7'6 x 9'6

LINEN
1'6 x 4'0

CLOSET
3'0 x 12'0

Flower Box

HALL
7'6 x 17'

BED ROOM
12'0 x 15'0

Flower Box

BED ROOM
12'0 x 15'6

Closet
4'6 x 5'0

Closet
4'6 x 5'0

BED ROOM
12'0 x 14'0

Flower Box

Second Floor Plan.   No. 720.

No. 721.

In this bungalow, under the direction of one with an appreciation of its possibilities, effects can be obtained by the use of clinker bricks and cobblestones that one could not wish bettered. Especially useful is this combination where it is desired to reconcile the difference between natural surroundings and the always more or less formal nature of architecture.

In this instance is exemplified its adaptability to overcoming a slight difference in grade, resulting in an effect that is pleasing and difficult to produce with masonry in horizontal courses. Shingles used on the walls give a rusticity that is in keeping with the unconventional clinkers and cobbles.

The interior is finished up with the latest bungalow ideas. This plan is 35x46 feet and will cost about $2,000.

Complete plans and specifications of this house, with all necessary details, either as shown on this page or reversed, will be furnished for $10.00.

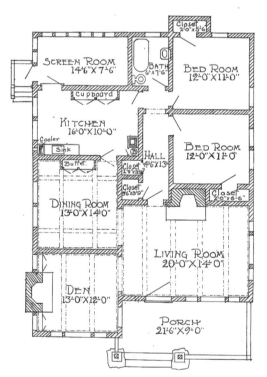

No. 722.

Clinker brick and cobblestones have been used with a satisfactory result for the porch masonry in harmony with the shakes. No illustration can give the beauty of materials of this nature; shakes or shingles when stained present beautifully mottled, variations of shades and the natural variety of tints in cobblestones and subtle contrasts in brick all contribute to a pleasingly varigated exterior that gives a bungalow the charm that cannot be equalled in the stately mansion, however resplendent with exquisite carving and expensive materials.

A cement porch floor and steps is used with propriety in this case. Very small expense is needed in the execution of the charming interiors.

If preferred, there may be two rooms finished in the attic. The dimension is 32x47, and it will cost about $1,850.

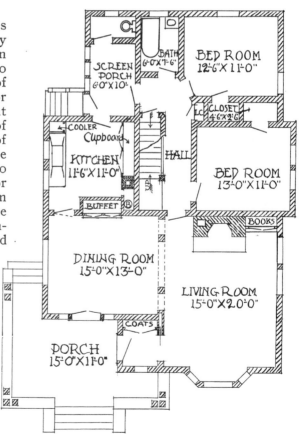

No. 723.

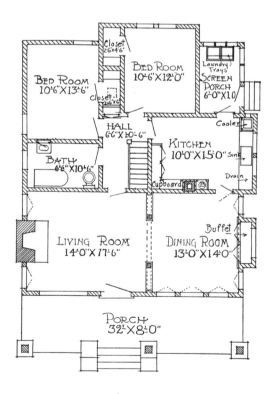

An artistic little bungalow is shown herewith; it would cost $1,600 and is 32x44. The living-room has a brick mantel of pleasing design. The dining-room buffet is located in the bay window, giving a desirable expanse of wall space.

The exterior is covered with resawed weatherboarding to belt course and shingles above. Has stone porch with cement floor.

Complete plans and specifications of this house, with all necessary details, either as shown on this page or reversed, will be furnished for $10.00.

No. 727.

This is one of our newest designs, which we believe will meet the approval of the readers of the Bungalow Book. Grace and lightness of line predominate in the external impression of this artistic home. The rafters and purlins penetrating the open verge board and eaves, give an original touch and show recognition of the principles of lightness in far projecting timbers or roofs. The frequent requests we receive for brick bungalows caused us to present the accompanying plan, which could be built with a solid brick wall or a brick veneer on a wood frame.

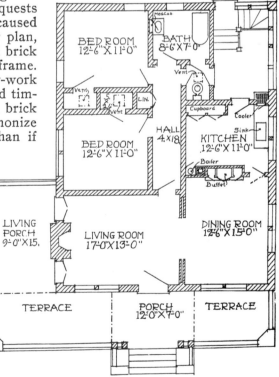

The delicate lines of the timber-work would admit of the use of dressed timber and painting in case pressed brick were used, which would harmonize better with such a treatment than if used with rough, stained exterior woodwork.

If dark red pressed brick were used, it would make a pleasing combination if the woodwork were painted a dull green. Asbestos makes a striking color note where used for a roof in a case like this.

This plan is 42 feet over all in width, which would admit of its being built on a 50-foot lot. The depth over all is 50 feet. It could be built at a cost of $2,100.

No. 728.

That concrete is not used more frequently in domestic architecture is due probably more to a lack of knowledge of its artistic possibilities rather than ignorance of its desirable qualities of sanitation, uniformity of temperature, and its cheapness when cost of repairs, painting and insurance enter into consideration.

The failure of many concrete designs, from the standpoint of esthetics, may be attributed to the coldness of effect resulting when there is nothing to replace the varied textures and mottlings of laid-up masonry.

In this design a frieze suggesting slightly a classic fretwork has made an opportunity to insert an enlivening touch of color.

If finished in the rough pebble dash, this should be executed with corresponding rusticity, using wide joints and irregularity of alignment in laying up the tile or brick used for the mosaic effect.

The smooth troweled finish would require more precise masonry and regular jointing of the mosaics.

Logical construction and beauty of timber-work marks the porch and pergola.

The trusses over the long spans possess both constructive and decorative functions.

An appreciation of the value of a straight line, independent of curves and ornament, and evidence of thoughtful study and instinctive taste in design are apparent in No. 728. The mode of subdividing the upper glass of the windows is in keeping with the spirit of the design, repeating the arrangement of the porch balustrade.

The floor plan is well considered. The originality of the exterior is repeated in the details of the interior, notably in the plastered fireplace and the buffet. The screen bedroom, by reason of its relation to kitchen and living-room, would serve equally well as a breakfast-room. On the second floor, the well-lighted hall gives immediate entrance to all bed-rooms and the bath.

The sewing-room could be used as a dressing-room in connection with the bed-room or as a child's bed-room. Large closets are included. This house covers an area 44x48 feet, including porches, etc. It would cost about $3,700.

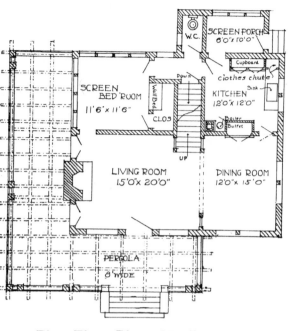

First Floor Plan. No. 728.

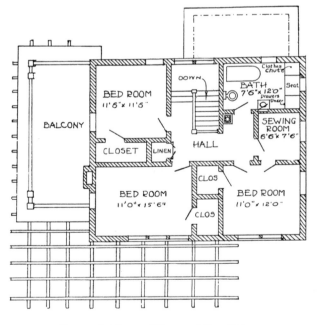

Second Floor Plan. No. 728.

Complete plans and specifications of this house, with all necessary details, either as shown on this page or reversed, will be furnished for $10.00.

No. 729.

No. 729 makes a very attractive house; the exterior is stucco to the belt course and shakes above laid in alternate courses of 4 and 9 inches to the weather. The front porch gives a very pleasing effect. It is partly covered and partly open, with rafter beams. It has a cement floor and steps.

The interior of this house is cleverly arranged. The living-room, dining-room and den are finished up with oak floors, panel wainscoting and beam ceilings; don't forget to notice the court on side, which is very desirable. The dimensions over all are 38x70 feet, and the estimated cost is $2,750.

Complete plans and specifications of this house, with all necessary details, either as shown on this page or reversed, will be furnished for $10.00.

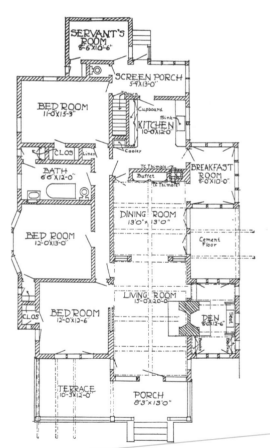

No. 731.

Massive solidity predominates in the proportions of this bungalow.

Ashlar stone work is used for the porch piers, foundation and chimney, harmonizing well with the light-colored trimming of the exterior.

Resawed siding covers the walls of the exterior; shingles are used in the gable.

An interesting element of the design is the flower box upon brackets under the shed roof in the front gable.

The den is provided with a combination seat and wall-bed, which gives all of the bed-room capacity of a house with three bed-rooms.

A feature of the dining-room is the serving ledge in the bay window, shown in this photograph. The total dimensions of this house are 30x57 feet. It cost $2,000.

Complete plans and specifications of this house, with all necessary details, either as shown on this page or reversed, will be furnished for $10.00.

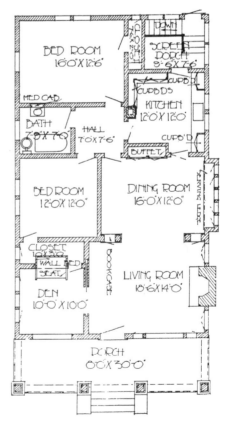

131

No. 733.

Two shades of artificial stone were used to obtain the effect of this masonry. The buttresses of the front steps were utilized as a pedestal for potted ferns.

Heavy hinges of wrought iron ornament the front door, which has three lights of bevel plate.

Half timber and plaster enriches the surfaces of the triple gable, which is the most striking feature of the front elevation of No. 733.

The chimney is built of the same ashlar that is used on the porch. Cement steps and floor are specified for the front porch and terrace.

Resawed siding is shown on the exterior. The interior is well arranged; particularly economical is the relation between the bath and kitchen. Large closets are provided for each of the three bed-rooms. 38x40 feet is the size of the main plan of this bungalow, which costs $1,800.

Complete plans and specifications of this house, with all necessary details, either as shown on this page or reversed, will be furnished for $10.00.

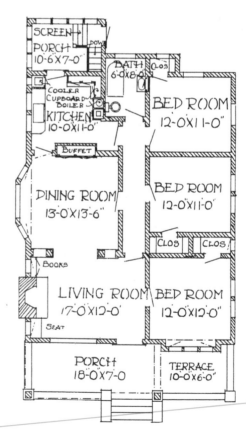

132

No. 734.

This one is somewhat different. The exterior is covered with vertical boards, and paneled with 2x6-inch timbers with 6x8-inch cross timbers at corners, the roof is covered with asbestos roofing; altogether this makes a very attractive and novel house; the dimensions are 38x26 feet and will cost about $1,500 to build.

Complete plans and specifications of this house, with all necessary details, either as shown on this page or reversed, will be furnished for $10.00.

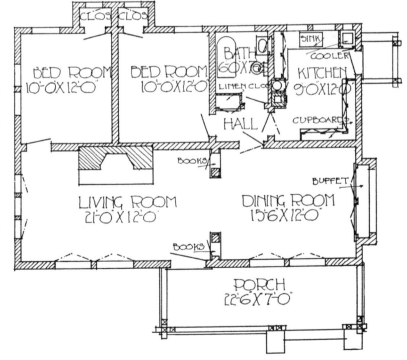

No. 735.

In this instance, shingles are laid in the gables, resawed rustic siding being used below.

Ashlar stone work is selected for the masonry of the porch.

An unusual touch is the fluting of the top course of stones, just beneath the projecting bases of the columns

The balustrade is built of the same artificial stone that is used for the pedestals of the columns.

With cement steps and floor this makes a very durable porch. The saving in painting and repairs will justify the additional first cost.

The dimensions are 28x42, and the estimated cost $2,250.

Complete plans and specifications of this house, with all necessary details, either as shown on this page or reversed, will be furnished for $10.00.

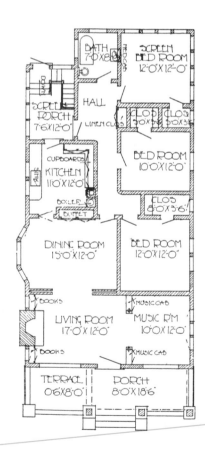

No. 736.

This simple and inexpensive little bungalow was built recently in Los Angeles. Below the belt course at the window sill resawed siding is used, flaring or "battering" out at the bottom to add an interesting base for the wall above which is shingled.

A neat design of wood muntins divides the glass of the windows.

The front door, which is not distinctly visible in this view, has three small bevel plate glass panels of uniform size, but stepping up in varying heights. The roof is supported by purlins ending at the verge boards, and the wall line except at intervals when they extend into the second rafter.

The wainscot in the dining-room consists of plaster panels divided by wood battens, each of which receives a bracket which supports the plate rail. The bed-rooms are finished in white enamel.

The plan is 25½x39 feet. It would cost $1,200.

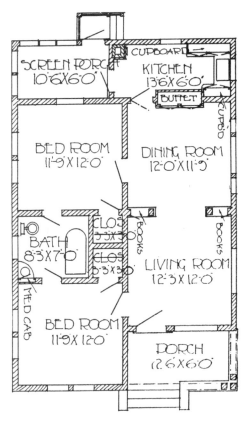

135

No. 737.

As shown in the photographic illustration, this bungalow was built on an inclined grade, incidentally showing a very good way to handle a situation of this kind.

If the weatherboarding of the front wall were continued instead of stopping at the porch stone work, it would give an unpleasant emphasis to the difference between the level boards and the decided slope of the ground. This difficulty is eliminated by the use of the irregular jointing, which forms a neutral transition from the horizontal lines to the slope of the grade.

This bungalow is 26x33, and the estimated cost is $1,050.

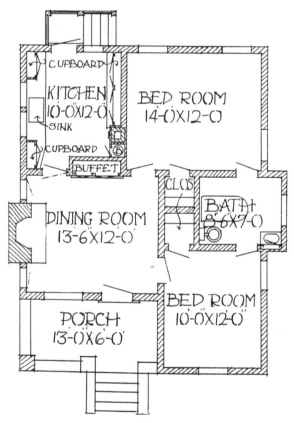

Complete plans and specifications of this house, with all necessary details, either as shown on this page or reversed, will be furnished for $10.00.

136

No. 738.

The ashlar coursed artificial stone with the cement steps and porch floor imparts an air of substantiality to this pleasing little bungalow.

Half-timber and plaster are introduced very successfully as a treatment of the gable over the front porch.

The house being stained brown for the body color, harmonizes well with the Naples yellow tint of the rough coat of plaster between the battens, which are white, the same as the remainder of the exterior trim.

The interior is simple and plain, but compact, and will cost about $1,600.

Complete plans and specifications of this house, with all necessary details, either as shown on this page or reversed, will be furnished for $10.00.

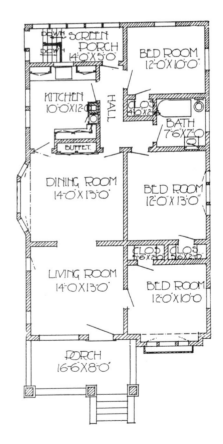

137

No. 739.

No. 739 is another odd and attractive design, and would make a home that would be admired by many. This bungalow has a cement porch floor, clinker brick, and the exterior trim is of unsurfaced material, which brings out a much desired effect. The interior shows a very clever arrangement of rooms, and is finished up in the latest styles and will cost about $2,000.

Complete plans and specifications of this house, with all necessary details, either as shown on this page or reversed, will be furnished for $10.00.

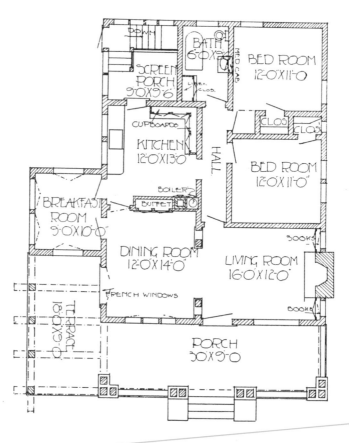

138

No. 741.

Double chains are hung between the stone piers, which form the pedestals of the columns.

This design, like No. No. 731, has the same peculiar elevation of the ends of the ridges that has been favorably commented upon by many who have seen the executed plan.

Shingles in r e g u l a r courses are specified on the main walls of the exterior; in the gables the shingles have been laid alternately short and long. This is very satisfactory.

This house is 36x44. The estimated cost is $1,980.

Complete plans a n d specifications of t h i s house, with all necessary details, either as shown on this page or reversed, will be furnished for $10.00.

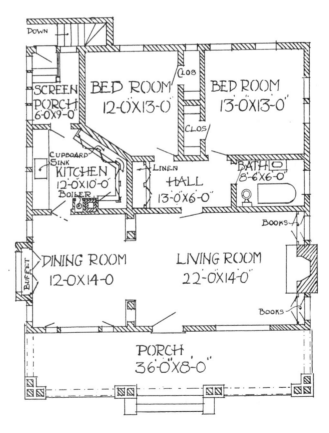

THE WILSON KITCHEN

Quite frequently we receive inquiries from readers of the Bungalow Book desiring information concerning details of certain parts of the Wilson bungalow, not clearly illustrated in the floor plans or exterior views.

For the benefit of those who have not had the opportunity to inspect a home executed in accordance with our plans, we will illustrate some features of the Wilson bungalow that would be of interest to the prospective builder.

First we show a view of the typical kitchen equipment of our bungalows.

Readers of the Bungalow Book are familiar with the usual kitchen plan, as arranged in the Wilson bungalow—characterized as the buffet plan; cupboards, equipped with shelves, drawers, coolers, draw bins and mouldboards filling all of the requirements in the modern culinary art, in a much less area than the old-fashioned pantry, or butler's pantry plan.

This means not only economy in building, but also a great saving of time and energy in the kitchen.

System is the secret of success of the giant enterprises of today that would bewilder the greatest business men of a few years ago who were unaided by the many devices and methods necessary to successfully conduct a comparatively small enterprise today.

The modern feminine mind is as quick to grasp the value of all devices that minimize the drudgery of housekeeping. Fewer hours spent in the kitchen, by the housewife of moderate means, makes possible more time for self-culture and benefiting others, in the library, music-room or nursery.

We are endeavoring to keep the kitchen of the Wilson bungalow up-to-date in every respect, and are always pleased to receive suggestions from any readers regarding possible improvements in any of the customary ways of arranging the plan of a home or any of its minor details.

The following illustrations will give some idea of the interior details of the Wilson bungalow. Any of these interiors will be incorporated in special plans if requested with order.

The Wilson Kitchen. See Opposite Page.

141

Interior, No. 551.

Interior View of Dining-Room, No. 629.

Interior of Dining-Room, No. 640.

Dining-Room, No. 658.

143

Living-Room, No. 719.

Interior View of Living-Room, No. 721.

Interior of Living-Room, No. 722.

Interior of Dining-Room, No. 727.

145

The Wilson Bath-Room.

Interior of a Hunting Lodge.

146

Interior of a Log Cabin.

Interior No. 1.

Interior No. 2.

Interior No. 3.

Interior No. 610.

Design in Dutch Clinker Brick, No. 600.

Interior No. 4.

Interior No. 5.

Dining-Room, No. 197.

Living-Room, No. 197.

Interior No. 118.

Interior No. 6.

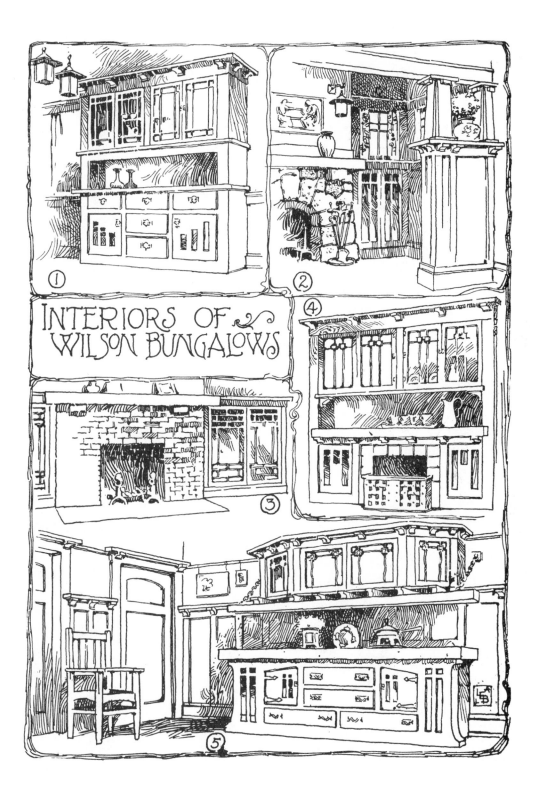

INTERIORS OF WILSON BUNGALOWS

153

Door No. 112.

Door No. 121.

Door No. 102.

Door No. 115.

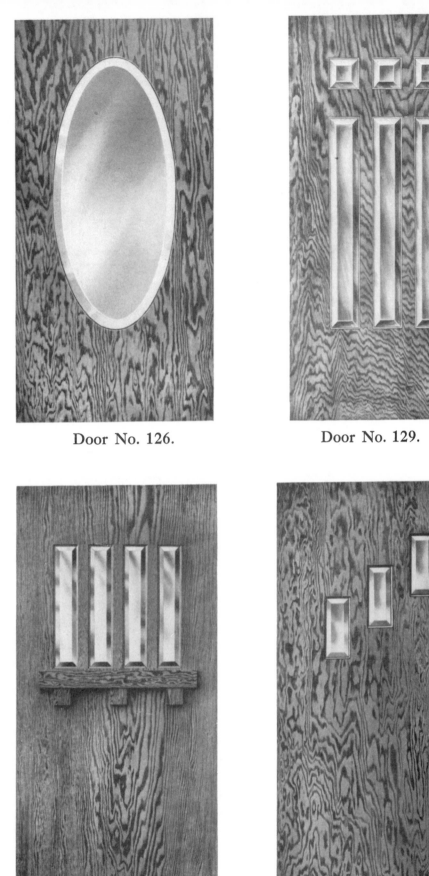

Door No. 126.

Door No. 129.

Door No. 132.

Door No. 135.

COMMENTS From a few purchasers of BUNGALOW PLANS

Bungalow Magazine,
Los Angeles, Cal.
Gentlemen:—
I have built from your plans, 572 and we are very much pleased with our new home, as we have the "biggest little" house in the city. We have had an endless shower of compliments and many enquiries as to where we got our plans.
I have never seen a poor plan in your magazine yet. I give all of my old copies away to people whom I think are interested, and urge them to subscribe even if they are going to build any style of house. Yours truly,
GEO. B. COOPER,
710 E. Washington St.,
Bloomington, Ill.

Oxnard, Cal., March, 1908.
"Plan for Bungalow came today, and is entirely satisfactory." J. R. GABBERT.
Oxnard, Cal.

Topeka, Kans. April, 1908.
"I received the plans and specifications and must say I am very much pleased with their completeness." H. C. STEVENS.
Topeka, Kan.

Calgary, Canada, May, 1908.
"Plans reached here yesterday and I can assure you that they are entirely satisfactory. I consider your charges most reasonable, and really had no idea when ordering the plans that they, together with the specifications would be so full and complete." H. A. ALLISON.
Calgary, Canada.

Rochester, Minn., June, 1908.
"Plans have arrived and we are delighted with them. The builders say they are the most complete they ever saw. A. W. BLAKELY.
Rochester, Minn.

San Francisco, Cal., June, 1908.
"Plans are at hand; they are proving very satisfactory." FRANK E. PARTMANN.
San Francisco, Cal.

Mr. H. L. Wilson,   St. Louis, Mo.
Los Angeles, Cal.
Dear Sir:—I am getting along nicely with my house built from your plan No. 151. I am much pleased with it. I will be able to use more of your plans in the future, as I am building and selling all the time. What price can you make on lots of six or more of the different designs shown in your Bungalow Book?
Awaiting your early reply, I am
Respectfully yours,
St. Louis, Mo.   C. H. WHITLEY.

Montgomery, Ala.
Mr. Henry L. Wilson,
Los Angeles, Cal.
Dear Sir:—I received the plans and specifications for my bungalow a week ago, and I have figures for building same for a few dollars less than your estimated cost. I am very much pleased with the plans. Yours truly,
GEORGE WATSON.
Montgomery, Ala.

South Berkeley, Cal.
Mr. H. L. Wilson, Architect,
Los Angeles, Cal.
Dear Sir:—I am getting along very nicely with the house so far and your plans have received many compliments from men well posted in cottages.
Yours truly,
JOHN NF. PRESTON.

Oakland, Cal., April, 1908.
"Plans and specifications received and we are very much pleased with them. You have received a great many compliments upon these plans."
JOHN M. HITCHINS.
Oakland, Cal.

San Mateo, Cal., July, 1908.
"I have just finished one of your houses (No. 167). I have worked in California for more than 18 years, and have never worked after a better plan. The house is the best looking house in Burlingame Park, and will prove a good advertisement for you, as well as for me."
San Mateo, Cal.   E. A. GORRILL.

Portland, Ore., July 25, 1908.
"I duly received your plans and specifications for my residence, and I am more than pleased with them. The house will be erected in the most fashionable district of this city, at No. 485 East Nineteenth Street North." SAM HICKS.
Portland, Ore.

Ventura, Cal., July, 1908.
"Your plan for Bungalow is in contractor's hands, who considers it most excellent and the explanations of details very clear." M. A. CUNNANE.
Ventura, Cal.

Los Angeles, Nov. 23, 1908.
Mr. Henry L. Wilson,
Los Angeles, Cal.
Dear Sir:—Plans and specifications No. 110 duly received and I am pleased with same. Herewith I hand you P. O. money order for $5, for which please send me, without delay, two duplicate sets of plans and specifications.
Very truly yours,
406 Union Trust Building.   W. A. HOWELL.

Oakland, Cal.
Mr. Henry L. Wilson,
Los Angeles, Cal.
Dear Sir:—Your plans Nos. 320, 392 and 356 with specifications came duly to hand yesterday by Wells-Fargo, and I wish to express my appreciation of their excellence.
I shall also want, later on, plans and specifications of your plan No. 394—46x36—that I think will suit another lot that I will likely build upon later. If you will include this one for $7.50 more, you may send it now. I hope to order a couple more in a month or two.
Again expressing my satisfaction with those already received, I remain
Yours respectfully,
GEO. W. KELLEY.
Care "The Piedmont Press," 1166 Weber St.,
Oakland, Cal.

ANNOUNCEMENTS CONCERNING STOCK PLANS

There being a large number of our clients who ask for lists of material and duplicate plans and specifications, we have decided to make the following offer:

The regular price of Ten Dollars covers the cost of one set of bungalow plans and specifications complete. For Fifteen Dollars we will furnish three complete sets of plans of any bungalow which we have published, including three sets of specifications and an accurate list of all materials, giving dimensions, that would be required in building. The convenience of having two extra plans and specifications would be worth the additional Five Dollars, while the material list might save ten times that amount in building.

SPECIAL PLANS

I wish to call attention to the fact that I am not confined to the sale of the enclosed plans, nor do I limit myself to the sale of drawings now in stock, inasmuch as I am fully prepared to incorporate your ideas in special work. If you wish to order special drawings, I would request that you inform me as to the locality in which you purpose to build, at the same time sending in your data as to the number of rooms and their arrangement, etc. For special plans, preliminary pencil sketches are always sent for criticism and alterations, and tracings are not completed until these sketches are approved.

The price for special plans will be five dollars per room for a house not costing over five thousand dollars. This price includes three duplicate sets of complete plans and specifications. First-story staircase halls or reception rooms, and basement each are counted as one room. Bath-rooms, screen porches, closets and interior halls or passageways are not counted as rooms.

A payment of one-third the total cost is required with the order for special plans. Call or send mail order to HENRY L. WILSON,

412 Copp Building,
    Los Angeles, Cal.

1412 Great Northern Building,
    Chicago, Ill.

Yours for Artistic Homes
Henry L. Wilson